YUM?

Interesting Origin Stories, Fun Facts, Questions & Answers, and Trivia About Food from Around the World

RIDDLELAND

INTRODUCTION

Every bite of food you eat has a history behind it. Those ingredients didn't just come together randomly on your plate; they are the result of something dramatic that happened in the past. This book shares those stories.

You might think the answer to where certain foods came from is obvious, but it's not. For instance, did you know Swiss Meatballs were not developed in Switzerland? Did you know that French fries didn't come from France? Would you believe that Great Britain is not the original home to either fish or chips? The Internet is full of blogs with people offering opinions – not facts, in many cases, just their personal beliefs of where foods originated, who created them, and why. Who should you believe?

This book attempts to get to the truth. It has been carefully researched using various Internet sites; all of these are in the back of the book in case you want to verify what you read in this book. Numerous sites have been examined, the most trustworthy ones have been identified, and all "facts" have been verified with at least one other source. That material has then been distilled into interesting articles that challenge you to name the food item discussed before the narrator reveals it.

Be prepared to be shocked. Among the many things you are going to discover in this book are

- There is no corn in corn beef.
- The Irish who live in Ireland do not eat corn, beef, and cabbage.
- There is a food named after gunpowder.
- Most movie theater owners in the early 1920s despised popcorn in their theaters.

The book covers a wide variety of foods and beverages. They are broken into categories such as appetizers, main courses, and desserts for reading ease. You can read the book cover to cover or use it as a reference to amaze your friends; for instance, the morning of the day that corndogs are going to be served in the cafeteria at lunch would be the perfect time to brush up on corndog facts. Although the book is written in a fun can-you-guess-what-it-is-before-I tell-you style, an index is provided so you can immediately go to the food item of your choice. This is a book you will want to refer to again and again.

So let's sink our teeth into some entertaining yet informative reading. The material is easy to digest, and you can always come back for seconds. This is one book that is truly in good taste.

TABLE OF CONTENTS

PART ONE:
BREAKFAST

CHAPTER 1

Prejudice and Pretzels Inspired This Treat

Have you ever gotten an unfair reputation because of your family? I know boys who are considered troublemakers just because their older brother is a troublemaker. It's not right to judge people before getting to know them, but – using family history, race, profession, religion, age, and other factors - most people make such judgments anyway.

Judging people without knowing them is nothing new. In the 1500s, Jews in Poland were considered enemies of the Christian Church. Almost 1500 years earlier, it was Jews who arranged for Jesus, the Christian Savior, to die on the cross, and since these Jews were the descendants of those people, the Christian population thought them to be enemies of the Church as well. The Jews were discriminated against in various ways, including what they could purchase and sell. Since Jesus had declared, "I am the bread of life," one of the restrictions on Polish Jews was that they could not bake bread.

Around 1500 C.E., a liberal Polish government decided that 1,500 years of discrimination was enough, and the government did away with the buying and selling restrictions previously imposed on the Jews. Unlike the government, though, the Polish Catholic Church was not ready to forgive and forget, and it argued to reinstate the restrictions. After much discussion, Church and the state agreed that Jews could buy ingredients and sell bread but that their bread could not be baked – it must be boiled.

The Polish Jews may have kept their Jewish religion and celebrated their Jewish heritage. Still, they realized that they lived within the Christian culture, and if they were going to be successful as merchants, they had to create products that Christians would buy. During Lent, making obwarzanek, a pretzel-like bread that didn't have eggs or milk, had become a tradition among Polish Christian bakers and the citizens of Poland – banned by the Church from eating meat as a sign they were fasting and trying to get right with God– they craved the baked bready treats.

The fact that the breads were baked kept the Jewish bakers from competing with the Christian bakers by offering an identical product. However, entrepreneurial Jewish bakers decided to enter the profitable market anyway; the Jewish bakers made the same product but boiled theirs as the regulations required. Whereas the pretzel was a three-holed bread that Christians said symbolized the Trinity - the Father, Son, and Holy Spirit, the Jewish bread was one loop and was said to represent eternal life. The first of these Jewish-baked rings were given to expectant mothers in Krakow in 1610, and the ring was thought to bring good luck in the birthing process and long life to the child.

The hole was not just a symbol meant to compete with the pretzel's three holes; it also had practical uses. The hole allowed the product to bake evenly, ensuring all the dough was cooked. It was also very practical; vendors could place the dough rings on a dowel rod and hock them on the streets.

When they migrated to the United States, Polish Jews brought their bread recipe of ringed dough with them. Like many foods, the bread got "Americanized," becoming softer and sweeter. However, the bread retained its hole and is now a common menu item on most fast-food breakfast menus. They don't call this bread with a hole in it an "obwarzanek," though; they call it the German word for "ring" **. . . the bagel.**

FUN FACTS

No other bread is boiled before it is baked.

The boiling heat causes the flour on the outer edge of the bread to create a water-tight coat – bagels float.

The more minerals contained in the water a bagel is boiled, the harder the bagel's shell will be.

CHAPTER 2
Name It and Claim It

I will be the first to admit that I have some weird friends. One of my friends likes to go to buffets, mix spaghetti with mashed potatoes, and then eat it. My guess is you have some weird friends too.

In 1974, a new restaurant opened in Santa Fe, New Mexico. It served spaghetti, no-bake cheesecake, and similar items. In 1975, it added a burrito to its breakfast menu. The burrito consisted of beef and potatoes wrapped in a tortilla shell – lots of potatoes, with optional eggs.

That probably doesn't sound like a big deal to you, and, in many ways, it was not. The burrito wrap was one of the first foods created in the North and South American continents; it was almost 4000 years old in 1975. Also, almost everything had been eaten on a burrito at one time or another. Beef and potatoes were certainly not a new combination.

What changed the world that day in 1975 was that the staff at Tia Sophia's recognized that potatoes and beef in a tortilla were worthy of being called a menu item. They put it on their menu, and they began to sell it. Their patrons loved it. Before long, other restaurants served burritos for breakfast, including fast food chains like McDonald's and Hardee's.

Think about a gold nugget in the middle of the street, washed from eroding soil during a rainstorm. Hundreds of people would walk by that gold nugget and leave it there, thinking it was just a rock. Eventually, someone would notice it and recognize its value. Similarly, people had seen the meat and potato burrito daily, but no one considered selling it in a restaurant. Tia Sophia, though, saw the value in it.

Tia Sophia's first burritos for breakfast were beef, potatoes, and optional eggs wrapped in a tortilla shell. However, people could add or subtract ingredients as they pleased. Today, Tia Sophia's breakfast burrito has evolved to be the customer's choice of bacon, ham, sausage, or bologna with potatoes and egg, wrapped in a flour tortilla and smothered with chili and topped with cheese; however, the staff will still be glad to make it however you like.

My friend has never come up with a name for her mashed potatoes and spaghetti mix; until she does, she won't sell it. Unlike other restaurants which saw people eating beef and potatoes in a tortilla shell and didn't name it and therefore couldn't sell it, when the personnel of Tia Sophia's saw it, they named it, and, by naming it, they were able to put it on the menu. The name of the item **. . . the breakfast burrito.**

FUN FACTS

Tia Sophia's has expanded beyond the breakfast burrito and now offers the breakfast enchilada, which consists of scrambled eggs and bacon wrapped in a corn tortilla, smothered in chili and cheese.

If a breakfast burrito is "smothered" in sauce, the sauce is outside the shell; if the breakfast burrito is "handheld," then the sauce is inside the burrito.

Tia Sophia's will make anything "Christmas," "Christmas" is slang for adding spicy red and green peppers.

Breakfast burritos outside the United States are often called "breakfast wraps."

CHAPTER 3
Four Dishes in One Bite

Human beings like routines; routines enable us to perform basic acts without putting too much thought into them. For instance, you likely have a morning routine; you do roughly the same thing every day, and if you skip a step, you feel like your whole day is off. For instance, I wake up, grab my cell phone and check for messages, get out of bed, go to the kitchen for breakfast, shave and brush my teeth, get dressed, and head off for classes. If I miss a step, such as not brushing my teeth, I feel paranoid about my teeth all day.

Since the 1600s, breakfast has been a part of people's morning routine. Breakfast likely began when the family farm started to decline, and the Industrial Revolution arose. Although farmers certainly had routines, they were not regimented like factory workers were. A farmer could pick an apple from one of his trees anytime; the factory worker had to eat at specified break times. The farmer could begin his day any time after sunrise; a factory worker had to be on the job at 7 a.m. sharp because so many other people depended on him. Farmers didn't eat what has become the traditional breakfast of bacon, pancakes, sausage, eggs, milk, and orange juice because they worked around food and they could take a snack break whenever they wanted; however, factory workers needed a large meal to sustain them throughout their long shifts, and they did not have the luxury of eating whenever they chose.

The appropriate time to eat breakfast has evolved; many restaurants now serve "breakfast" all day. When the concept of breakfast began, breakfast foods were accepted as early morning foods. The term "breakfast" literally means to break one's fast, that is, one's not eating. Society deemed certain foods appropriate for breaking the fast since one's evening meal. Although technology inspired some additions – the technology to make Corn Flakes, Rice Crispies, and most other cereals was not developed until the early 1900s – bacon, eggs, sausage, and bread became the core breakfast items.

Breakfast has become regarded as the most important meal of the day; people need to run on good nutrition just like machines need good energy sources. However, the idiom "an object in motion tends to stay in motion" and its opposite, "an object at rest tends to stay at rest," applies to humans. People who are awake often have a hard time going to sleep, and people who are waking up tend to have difficulty getting themselves motivated. This means that people are constantly leaving things to the last possible minute. That extra five minutes of sleep may feel great, but one must hurry to compensate for lost time. These procrastinators did not have time to sit down to a hearty breakfast – but they still needed to eat, and they still needed to be to work on time.

It seemed like an impossible situation – how could one sleep late and still enjoy a good breakfast, but a smart cook – likely a spouse of a factory worker or a cook for workers on the transcontinental railroad, came up with a solution. This unknown heroine or hero remembered how the Earl of Sandwich had put meat between pieces of bread so that he wouldn't get his fingers dirty playing cards. She decided to resolve the procrastinators' breakfast-eating dilemma similarly. She placed the eggs, bacon, and cheese inside the bread and then handed the sandwich to the procrastinator to eat while running to work.

The idea spread quickly, and over 140 years later, thousands of people grab a biscuit, muffin, or bagel with egg, cheese, and/ or meat on it to this day. In fact, in the United States, fast food restaurants have popped up that will hand you a biscuit, muffin, or bagel sandwich as workforce members drive by their window on the way to their jobs. Over in Europe, the sandwich was called a Bap Sandwich, named after the type of bread that was originally used. It has been called a biscuit sandwich in the United States, even if it was a muffin or bagel. Some restaurants have branded their sandwich product, such as McDonald's, calling it Canadian bacon, cheese, and egg in a McMuffin. The official name, though, is so generic that it encompasses all forms of bread and any breakfast ingredient one might want; it's called **. . . the breakfast sandwich.**

FUN FACTS

Jack in the Box was the first fast food restaurant to offer a breakfast sandwich in 1969. Breakfast sandwiches, though, didn't become popular at fast food restaurants until the introduction of the Egg McMuffin at McDonald's in 1971.

The first recipe for the breakfast sandwich appeared in an 1897 cookbook by Maud Cooke, *Breakfast, Dinner, and Supper: What to Eat and How to Prepare It.*

Scientists have concluded that breakfast is the most important meal of the day.

CHAPTER 4

The Food that Launched a Thousand Ships

You have probably heard of the Spanish explorer Ferdinand Magellan, the captain of the first expedition that sailed around the world. (He died on the journey, but part of his crew returned to port.) Most people realize he wanted to sail around the world, but have you ever wondered why he wanted to sail around the world? To prove that the world was round is a partially correct answer, but most royalty wouldn't sponsor an expedition just for science. Do you want to know what the practical reason was?

Magellan was tasked with sailing to new lands to find a new source of a secret spice. This incredibly valuable spice had been around since ancient Egypt, and Egyptians had used it for mummifying their dead rulers. Ancient Greeks used it as an incense offering to the gods, especially Apollo. It had been more precious than salt or pepper, two very precious spices in the

Roman Empire. (People used to get paid in salt; that's where the idiom "worth his salt" came from.) This spice, though, was so precious that only those in the emperor's inner circle had access to it.

Those who traded in the spice knew they had a real treasure, so they were careful never to reveal their source. Between wooing and threats, Spain and other countries had tried to get these traders to reveal the spice's native land, but the merchants would not talk. The leads the Spanish had obtained, such as the spice being brought up from the bottom of the Nile, had not panned out. By 1519, Spanish leadership had decided that if the merchants were not giving up the location, they would find a second location and claim it for Spain. They, therefore, invested heavily in exploring the uncharted and unexplored territories of the New World.

Fortunately for us, they found the spice, and it became so common that even cash-strapped peasants could enjoy it. While it was still relatively scarce but abundant enough that the wealthy could afford it, it was used as a cough suppressant; the spice was known for its healing qualities. Those who took it for medicine couldn't help but notice that it tasted great, and people began to eat it for the joy of its taste. One of the most popular recipes for it was to put it on bread with butter and sugar. Word of how to apply this spice to bread traveled rapidly by mouth and cookbook. This spice became so common that making spiced bread was cheaper than making traditional French toast.

Recipes for making the spiced bread vary slightly. Some say to add the spice, butter, and sugar before cooking the bread; others say to do it after; and some even suggest doing it both ways, allowing the sugar to caramelize. For over 600 years, this tasty treat has been a part of many breakfasts; in 1984, General Mills even introduced a cereal that mimics this taste. Not only is this taste loved by children and adults when they have a healthy appetite but it is also served to people when they are too sick to eat full-course meals. When your stomach is a bit queasy, don't be surprised if your mom offers you . . . **cinnamon toast.**

FUN FACTS

Although the spice merchants would not tell where they were getting cinnamon from, we know today that it was from Bangladesh, India, Myanmar, and Sri Lanka, with Egypt serving as a distributing hub.

Cinnamon-like spices have been found in China, Vietnam, Indonesia, New Zealand, and other Southeast Asian countries.

Cinnamon was first used in China around 2800 B.C.E.

The typical cinnamon tree stands at 60 feet.

The official name for a stick of cinnamon is "a quill."

CHAPTER 5
Devouring the Moon

In 1683, the residents of Vienna, Austria, had a problem. The Ottoman Empire was expanding, and their city was one of the places the empire sought to claim. Rather than conduct an all-out frontal attack on the city and lose thousands of its soldiers, the Ottoman Empire surrounded the city so that no one could get in or out. The residents had refused to surrender for two months, but now supplies were running low. The situation appeared hopeless, with morale and food running at an all-time low.

The siege was also tough on the Ottoman soldiers; they were bored. Concluding that the Vienna citizens were malnourished and weak, the Ottomans decided to tunnel under the walls and open the city gates to the army. A baker, though, was working late one evening, and he overheard Ottomans outside the city wall talking about the tunnel. He promptly alerted the authorities about the existence of the tunnels, and they, in turn, shared the intelligence with their army. With this information, the Austrians were able to capture the tunnels and force the Ottomans to flee.

To celebrate the victory, the baker created crescent-shaped roles. In Islam, the crescent-shaped moon symbolizes the Day of Judgment, and the victory had been the day of judgment against the Islamic land grab. The villagers ate the crescent moon-shaped pastry, reminding them of how their army had swallowed the Ottoman army.

The crescent-shaped pastry might never have been heard of outside of Vienna, though, if it wasn't for a 14-year-old girl named Marie. Marie was an Austrian princess who loved those crescent moon-shaped pastries. Royal children often wed with royal children in other countries as a sign of alliance – not because they loved each other; so, at 14, this Vienna princess married the future French King, Louis XVI, and went to Paris to live with him. Paris differed from Austria in many ways, and she longed for food from her native Austria. Her request for the crescent pastry was granted, and they became a staple of the French court. Because the French court began to serve them to foreign dignitaries, the crescent moons began to be referred to as a French dish.

Marie would later become more famous for another food item – cake. That's right, the 14-year-old girl who introduced the croissant pastry to the world outside Vienna was Marie Antoinette, the French queen who, when she heard there was a food shortage among the peasants, nonchalantly declared, "Let them eat cake." Meanwhile, she kept eating the crescent-moon-shaped pastry she called "kipfel." Once in the French court, it became known outside of France as the French croissant, or as we call it today, the **. . . croissant.**

FUN FACTS

Although croissants began as a food of the rich, they soon became the food of the middle class, and the rich moved on to brioche.

Ever since 1920, the croissant has been the official product of France.

Before the croissant, puff pastry was either used as a shell or a garnish; it was not intended to be eaten.

CHAPTER 6
The Hole Story

Do you like to eat while you work?

Hanson Gregory, an American sea captain from Camden, Maine, sure did. One of his favorite things to eat was the fried dough ball, called "olie koeken" or "olykoeks", translated into English as an oil cake, a cake deep fried in hog fat. His Dutch ancestors had brought the recipe from the Netherlands when they had migrated to the United States beginning in the late 1600s, and he frequently took the small dough balls with him on his voyages.

He typically steered the ship with one hand and reached for the fried dough ball with his other hand. One day in 1847, though, when the sea suddenly turned especially choppy, he needed both hands on the wheel. Not having a place to set the fried dough ball he was about to bite into, he impaled it on a spoke of the steering wheel.

Gregory looked at the impaled dough ball. One of the problems with the dough ball was that it had to be kept small in shape because if it had been large, the center would not cook through before the outside was completely cooked. Cooks solved this problem by hollowing out most dough balls with large middles and replacing the missing dough with nuts or jam. As Gregory stared at the impaled, flattened dough ball, he realized that if he put a hole in the center and flattened the ball, the product would cook evenly throughout.

He asked a tinsmith to create a device to create holes in dough balls and had the ship's cook test his idea. The device successfully removed the middle, making the pastry into a ring. The cook then fried the ring as usual, and the resulting product tasted wonderful. Unlike the knots of dough, which were often undercooked or grease-logged, this product had cooked perfectly. He was so proud of what he had done that he sent a batch of the result to his mother in Rockport, Maine, and she quickly shared it with her friends. Word quickly spread about these unique dough knots, but instead of calling the dough knots, people referred to them as . . . **doughnuts.**

FUN FACTS

The National Baking Association has nominated Hanson Gregory for the Baking Hall of Fame, but he has not yet been accepted.

Adolph Levitt, a Russian immigrant to the United States, created the first doughnut-making machine in 1920.

Doughnuts were showcased at the 1934 Chicago World's Fair. This exposed people worldwide, particularly in the United States, to the taste sensation of the doughnut.

In the 1930s, dunking doughnuts became a fad.

CHAPTER 7

The Little Cakes with a Big Reputation

Sometimes it is not just great tastes that make a food famous; sometimes, it is good advertising and product placement. Numerous food concoctions have been developed in kitchens worldwide, but because of a lack of advertising, no one aside from a close circle of family and friends has ever heard of it or tried it. In other cases, such as New Coke by the Coca-Cola Company, a product is heavily hyped and strategically placed. Still, if it does not taste well, no amount of hype will keep people purchasing it again and again. In some cases, though, a great product meets great advertising and great placement, and it not only takes off but remains popular for centuries.

This is the case with "little cakes." Little cakes were first mentioned in 1703; they were small, round, flat cakes that could be eaten in a single sitting. Little cakes were consumed with butter and jam on them. Rich people had ovens and could cook their own little cakes; a cookbook with the recipe was published in 1747. However, poor people could not afford an oven and had to rely on the local bakery.

An enterprising man saw the profit potential. He bought numerous little cakes from the local bakery, then wandered the streets with them in his basket, selling one to anyone asking. Just in case someone was oblivious to him, he rang a handheld bell and shouted what he had to sell. His business was so successful that many others started to copy his formula for success on other streets in London, selling little cakes to those families who could not make their own.

An English immigrant, Samuel Thomas, exposed the United States to little cakes in 1780 when he opened a bakery in New York City. A nearby hotel bought his little cakes, which he called "toaster crumpets," and sold them to guests as an alternative to toast. The little cakes were a hit. Of course, by the time they found success in the United States, they were no longer called "little cakes." Instead, they were called the German word for little cakes, "muffin," and to distinguish them from American muffins, which were – and still are - more like cupcakes, these little cakes were called . . . **the English muffin.**

FUN FACTS

The English muffin is more popular in the United States than in England.

The inside of an English muffin looks like a honeycomb; this sponge-like texture is great for soaking up butter.

The nursery rhyme "The Muffin Man" was written no later than 1820 in honor of the men who walked around the lower-class neighborhoods of London ringing their handheld bells and selling muffins. There really was a Drury Lane, too, where he might have lived; it was in the poor part of London.

CHAPTER 8
A True Masterpiece

What do comic strips, Campbell's soup cans, and posters of Marilyn Monroe have to do with breakfast? Probably more than you think.

Beginning in the mid-1950s, a new art form emerged in the United States and Great Britain. Artists from the stuffy world of fine art started to paint pictures of everyday art found in popular culture. You may never have thought of it, but that Campbell's soup label is a work of art. So is that picture in the comic book. When Andy Warhol, Tom Wesselmann, Roy Lichtenstein, and numerous others started painting these everyday objects, they began the art movement known as Pop Art.

At about the same time, Ron Deluca, a Kellogg's employee, was tasked with creating a breakfast pastry. Post, Kellogg's biggest rival in breakfast food sales, had just announced the creation of "Country Squares," a toasted pastry that they planned to release. In 1963, Post developed the technology to keep fruit flavors from spoiling if not refrigerated, and this meant their product would keep for a long time, just like their cereal. (Nobody wants to bite into a pastry and get a bite full of mold.) Post said that the warm pastry would complement a cold breakfast of its cereal; too, the delicious fruit-filled pastry could also be a portable handheld breakfast for kids running late to school. The product was not ready for release yet, and Kellogg's saw the opportunity to fill the void Post had discovered.

Deluca worked closely with Bill Post, head of the Keebler bakery, and together they took some strawberry fruit filling and placed it between two layers of rectangular crust. The product was then precooked and wrapped in a plastic bag. Deluca called the product the Fruit Scone. By the time the product was test marketed in Cleveland in 1964, they had created three other flavors: apple currant, blueberry, and brown sugar cinnamon. Today, there are over 27 flavors, including raspberry, grape, and hot fudge sundaes.

The pastry evolved over the years. In 1967, a frosting could be toasted; in 1968, even sprinkled sugar could be applied to it before it was toasted. As the pastry evolved, so did its name. The Fruit Scone was a masterpiece, and so Kellogg's decided to rename it in honor of pop art; they called it the . . . **Pop-Tart.**

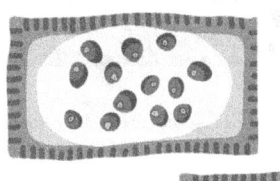
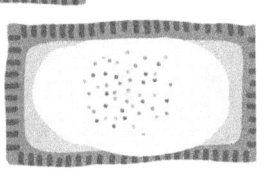

FUN FACTS

Pop-Tarts are flammable. If left in the toaster too long, they will catch fire.

Although Kellogg's Pop-Tarts has twenty standard flavors, such as strawberry, it has about ten experimental flavors on the market at any given time; in most cases, these are soon retired, and another experimental attempt is tried. Meanwhile, some flavors appear annually for a brief period, such as pumpkin pie flavor appears each autumn.

As part of its original marketing for Pop Tarts, Kellogg's insisted grocers place them in the baking aisle, far away from the cereal aisle, believing they would stand out more there.

Although a brand name, the term "pop tarts" is often used as a generic term to describe any rectangular, flat pastry with jelly or jam; thus, many restaurants serve homemade and pre-packaged pop tarts that are not Kellogg's Pop-Tarts.

When Pop-Tarts were launched, Milton the Toaster, a cartoon mascot created by Kellogg's, spread the word about Pop-Tarts on children's shows.

After learning that people were crumbling their Pop-Tarts and adding milk, Kellogg's introduced Pop-Tart cereal in 1994.

CHAPTER 9
The First Processed Food

Pause for a moment and look at any food item in your canned goods area or at any meat in your refrigerator that you got from the grocery store. The chances are that you will find that you are getting your product, a piece of meat or a canned peach, but you are also getting something else, a lot of preservatives. Preservatives are added to food products to enable them to last longer and protect them from dangerous molds and bacteria that could harm the consumers' health.

Although people take canneries and meat processing plants for granted today, our prehistoric ancestors were hunters and gatherers who had to eat their food on the spot or risk bacteria setting in. Have you ever wondered what was the first processed food and how it was processed?

As you might suspect, the first thing to be preserved was

meat. Whereas unused berries could be left on the bushes and unused vegetables left in the ground until the next day, when an animal was harvested, it had to be harvested in its entirety to prevent spoilage.

Meat processing dates back over 4,000 years. A tablet found in Mesopotamia, modern Iran, and Iraq describes how to process meat. Meat was processed to extend its life and allow people to transport it from one location to another. The Mesopotamians would use sheep intestines to place scraps and shavings of meat and then use salt to keep the meat fresh. When people settled into farming instead of being nomads, most villages had a butcher, a person who was an expert at cutting and preserving meat. By packing the intestinal casing tightly with the meat slivers he would otherwise have thrown away, the butcher could enhance his profit, be a better steward of the environment and reduce food storage.

Although most of us don't think of it as eating an intestine – that kind of thought could turn many people into vegans, this meat product is still very popular. Today, the meat casing may be an animal intestine, but it could also be synthetic. In many cases, bread, grain, and other extenders are added to the meat, salt, and spices before being stuffed into the sleeve. Whether it is beef, poultry, or chicken, this resulting meat product is still referred to by the word for "seasoned with salt," we call it **. . . sausage.**

FUN FACTS

No two sausages are alike. Not only do they have different spices, but they also have a different percentage of the animal's body parts comprising them.

In the Middle Ages, it was customary for the butchers to receive the head, hide, and offal of the butchered animal as partial payment, just as we tip waiters and waitresses today.

The spices mixed with meat to create sausage can also be mixed with plants to create a vegan sausage that tastes very similar to traditional sausage.

PART TWO:

APPETIZERS

BEVERAGES

AND SIDES

CHAPTER 10
His Borderline Salad was Anything but Borderline

Borderlines are literally lines on the dirt. In many cases, you will pay a heavy tax on one side of the line, and on the other, you will pay a light one. Many people come to my state because our gasoline has less tax than their state charges. Similarly, you can do something on one side of the line; on another, you can't. For instance, in my state, you can sell fireworks; in a bordering state, you cannot. That invisible line greatly affects how people can and cannot behave.

No one knew this better than restaurateur Cesare Cardini. Cesare was an Italian immigrant who had come with his family to the United States to make a living. He was a good chef and made a good living in his restaurant

33

in San Diego until Prohibition passed, stopping the sale of alcohol. In Cesare's restaurant, alcohol had been a high-profit item, so his business sales suffered.

Cesare knew that turning to organized crime for alcohol was a route many were taking, but he was highly ethical and pragmatic. He realized Prohibition didn't exist across the nearby borderline, so he opened a restaurant in Tijuana, Mexico. Although located in Mexico, his clientele was mostly well-to-do Americans who drove or took commuter flights.

On the Fourth of July in 1924, his restaurant was so bombarded with Americans on holiday that he ran out of many restaurant supplies. Late in the day, another large group of Americans walked through the door. Not wanting to turn away the guests, Cesare invited them to partake of a special salad; it's likely not even he knew what would be in the salad. He was an Italian chef who lived in America but was working in Mexico and fed Americans with ingredients from Mexico. He stalled the guests while his cooks raided the cupboards, pantries, and nearby stores for ingredients.

If Cesare had any doubts about the resulting product being tasty, he didn't show them. He began tossing the salad in front of the guests with great fanfare. He had made a popular "insalata mista" before and planned to parallel it with the ingredients on hand. He took whole Romaine lettuce leaves, coddled eggs, garlic-infused olive oil, croutons, Parmesan cheese, lemon juice, and Worcestershire sauce and mixed them all together. This was the best salad many of these customers ever had, and it became a requested item. It wasn't just the salad the customers liked; they loved the dressing too. He quickly trademarked the dressing and, by 1935, was marketing bottles of it.

Over time, people added and subtracted an ingredient here and there to suit their taste or the taste of their clients, but, to this day, many restaurants carry a salad modeled after what Cesare made. Although he spelled his name, Cesare, he didn't protest when the world changed the spelling when they named the salad in his honor, calling it the **. . . Caesar salad.**

FUN FACTS

The Caesar salad was nicknamed the Aviator Salad in honor of the pilots who flew Americans across the border.

The prohibition of alcohol production, transportation, and sales ran from January 1929 until December 1933. It took a Constitutional Amendment to start Prohibition and a Constitutional Amendment to end the 18th and the 21st, respectively. Although Prohibition ended at the federal level in 1933, individual states, counties, and towns can still regulate alcohol sales.

Julius Caesar, Caesar Augustus, nor any of the other Roman leaders ever had a Caesar salad.

CHAPTER 11
Saving the Shaving

Do you whittle? Whittling is when you take a knife and shave off pieces of wood or soap to create a statue. Whittling leads to a lot of waste; scraps and shavings are everywhere. Imagine you oversaw workers who whittled thousands of statues daily; think about how many shavings would be on the ground, likely to be swept up and thrown away. Now, think about how much money you would save if you could somehow put all those scraps and shavings back into a whole again.

Chicken processing plants were having a similar problem. They were leaving scraps and shavings behind when they prepared a chicken. They realized if there was a way to combine all these small pieces into a bigger, edible piece, they could be better stewards of the environment, reduce food shortages by allowing a chicken to feed more people, and keep more chickens for reproducing. In the 1970s, Americans had become concerned about eating too much red meat, so Americans were looking for an alternative to beef; the demand for chickens was up, and finding a way to salvage the scraps and shavings of harvested birds would meant the processing plant could increase their profit per chicken.

A way to do this had been discovered in the 1950s by Robert Baker, a Cornell University food science professor, but no one was interested in his work then. Using salt, grains, milk, and vinegar, he had found a batter that could be frozen and fried, keeping the small chicken shavings together. He called his invention the Chicken Crispie.

In the late 1970s, McDonald's Restaurants was looking for an alternative menu option to beef, and Tyson Food created a recipe for them relying on Baker's technology. In 1979, the first Chicken McNugget appeared and was a hit with the test market. Seeing how well the product fared in the test market and fearing they could not keep up with demand, the two companies waited until 1983 to launch the fried nuggets nationwide.

Cooked in vegetable oil, the McDonald's nuggets were offered as a healthy alternative to beef. To assure people that they were not eating gross byproducts, McDonald's promoted the nuggets as pieces of meat from the breast and thigh – which they were; they were just tiny shaved pieces instead of the traditional one-piece. The marketing worked, and Chicken McNuggets quickly became a part of American fast-food culture.

Seeing McDonald's success, competitors and home cooks wanted to cook nuggets too. Baker's technology was unpatented; therefore, competitors could not use McDonald's patented recipe, but they could use Baker's technology and develop their own recipe. Of course, the only place to get Chicken McNuggets is McDonald's, and it is a unique recipe no one else has. However, numerous other recipes have been created from Baker's technology. These other places don't call their product the Chicken Crispie, and they certainly don't call it a McNugget; instead, chicken shavings held together by a fried batter are called **. . . chicken nuggets.**

FUN FACTS

There is no part of a chicken known as "the nugget."

McDonald's has made a McNugget out of beans; it sells it in select restaurants as a Garden McNugget.

To be accepted as a McNugget, the food item can have one of only four different shapes.

The typical chicken nugget is only 50% meat; the rest is breading, stray chicken parts, and chemicals holding the meat parts together.

CHAPTER 12
The Energizing Berries

Kaldi was an Arab boy tending goats on his father's fields in Ethiopia; well, he was supposed to be tending goats. Like many children, he had gotten momentarily distracted watching a nearby bird land in the tree above him. He had moved just in time to avoid getting hit by the bird's deposit. As he stood up to protest the bird's actions, the bird flew away. He brushed himself off and realized his goats had gone grazing over the hill without him.

He hurriedly climbed the nearby hill and saw the goats below. These goats looked like his goats – he was sure they were his goats, but they acted very differently than his goats normally acted. His goats were calm, in fact, outright boring. These goats, though, were dancing and frisking about the field. What happened, he wondered.

He watched the goats and noticed that those goats eating the red-berried plants had a huge energy boost. Seeing the plant was the source of their energy and that it wasn't killing the goats, he also decided to eat the berries. He had experienced a very boring day so far and was curious if he, too, would have boundless energy and joy.

Having eaten a few berries, he was shaking and full of energy. He had been in this field many times before but had never seen the red-berried plant. He wondered how they had magically appeared, but then he remembered which had almost pooped on his head; he recalled that birds often pooped berry seeds. Now he knew how the plant got there – he just didn't know what it was. Curious about what he had found, he left the goats in the field and ran to the village's wisest, most educated monks.

Between his enthusiasm and the chemicals in the red berries, Kaldi was hyperactive. He picked a handful of berries and then ran to the village monks, who urged him to sit down and calm down. He tried, but he couldn't stop shaking, and he could not stop speaking hurriedly. Finally, the head monk said, "Enough," and tossed Kaldi's sample berries into the fire. "These are of the devil!"

The berries fell into the fire, creating a sweet aroma within moments. The head monk wanted to enjoy the aroma for days, so he ordered the burning berries to be pulled out and put into water to cool down so they could be used another day. A couple of monks tasted the water now that the hot berries were in it; they felt relaxed and soon noticed they could stay awake longer than their peers. The head monk declared that these berries should be the monastery's property, for they helped the monks study and feel God's presence.

Were the monks of this town able to keep the secret for almost 650 years? Perhaps they did - or perhaps there is another story of discovery, but around 1400, the beverage began to be well-known in society. As the legend suggests, when first introduced, it was drunk by the priesthood and the wealthy; no one else could afford it. The legend is also correct in saying that the beverage originated in Ethiopia and the Ottoman Empire and then spread to the rest of the world through trade. Today, the bean is widely grown, and the price has fallen, so anyone can enjoy it. It is a breakfast drink, a refreshing mid-morning beverage, and a late-night study buddy.

The beverage became so commonplace that the average person – the average Joe, would drink it, and it was affectionately nicknamed "a cup of Joe" by Americans in the late 1910s. The original monks and today's society as a whole, though, call it . . . **coffee.**

FUN FACTS

Brazil produces more coffee beans than any other country.

Many coffeehouses and cafes reference the founding legend, naming their restaurant after Kaldi or giving it a goatlike reference, such as "Wandering Goat."

Starbucks, headquartered in Seattle, Washington, is the largest coffee chain in the world. The name Starbucks was chosen because the restaurant's founders thought it would remind people of the sea-faring adventures of the early coffee traders.

CHAPTER 13
The Delicious White Lie

Where do you want to go on vacation? Do you want to go to a city like New York City? Paris? London? How about going to a country like China? Jamaica? Spain? Would you rather go to a landmark like the Egyptian pyramids? The Grand Canyon? The Amazon Rainforest? Wherever it is, I bet you have grand visions of the place.

You probably wouldn't want to go if you didn't have grand visions of the place. However – not that I want to be a Doubting Debbie and ruin your day- your visions are probably inaccurate. You will find that the place you are traveling to will be much worse than you think. New York, Paris, and London have slums, noise, and crime. The Grand Canyon is dusty and hot; the Amazon Rainforest is muggy and humid.Believe it or not, most people who live in your vacation spot may look forward to taking a vacation themselves, perhaps coming to where you call home.

Travel agencies sell fantasies; restaurants do too. Most foreign restaurants you visit do not offer the countries' native food; they offer what you think they eat in their native country. That, in turn, solidifies your belief that you were right in your knowledge of their culture all along.

Victor Bergeron was a master at selling the illusion. In 1934, he opened Trader Vic's, a Polynesian-themed restaurant. Most of his customers had never been to the Orient, but they had ideas of what it would be like. Some would call it stereotyping and racism, but Victor gave them the paradise they wanted. He decorated with Polynesian artifacts, served Polynesian cocktails – well, at least they were inspired; Victor invented the Mai Tai and a couple of others- and served so-called Polynesian food. Although Vic's prices were high, people flocked to Trader Vic's, an island-themed restaurant, and his one location soon turned into many.

In the 1950s, Victor served crab dumplings with cream cheese in his restaurants. Most people in the United States knew that crab was a large part of the Polynesian diet. Most people in the United States did not realize that cream cheese is not a large part of the Polynesian diet; the Americans tended to assume that since cream cheese is a part of American and European diets, then it was of Polynesians' diets as well. His patrons thought they were eating an ancient treat; they didn't realize Victor had just made it up. It was so popular, though, that Thai and Chinese restaurants, many of which already served Americanized versions of their native meals, also began to sell this "native" product, which helped to establish the Polynesian roots of Vic's product even more.

To lend authenticity to his new food, Victor called it Rangoon Crab; Rangoon was a city in Burma. (Perhaps Rangoon did have a recipe for crab dumplings, but it certainly would not have called for cream cheese.) In addition to Rangoon Crab, the product went by various other names, such as crab pillows, cheese wontons, crab puffs, and crab cheese wontons. In a Polynesian/Oriental restaurant, any of these terms may get you the dish, but the accepted name for the dish today is the name Victor chose – but in the opposite order . . . **Crab Rangoon.**

FUN FACTS

Trader Vic's string of tiki bars inspired Joe Coulombe to name his grocery store chain Trader Joe's. Joe wanted people to remember that both had great food but that Joe's prices were much lower than Vic's.

In addition to the Mai Tai and Crab Rangoon, Victor also invented the poupou platter, sometimes called po-po, of appetizers, an assortment of meat and seafood appetizers on one plate.

Cream cheese was invented around 1873 in New York City.

CHAPTER 14

The Potato Reimagined

Have you ever walked by something every day and thought it was being put to great use, and then, one day, a stranger walks up who does not know the current use and proceeds to give it a brand new use? That happened to me on my smartphone. I thought I was playing an app how it was supposed to be used; I let my friend borrow my phone, and he proceeded to do something else with it – something I had never thought of doing.

The same thing has happened with food products too. The potato was the first crop South Americans, notably the Mayans, in Peru and Bolivia planted. Archeologists have found potato-planting tools that go back to at least 3800 B.C.E.; written records prove the potato was domesticated by 2000 B.C.E. Needless to say, with over 9,500 years of experience growing, harvesting, and consuming the potato, the Mayans were confident they knew all there was to know about the potato.

Beginning with Christopher Columbus in 1492, Spanish explorers began to acquaint themselves with the North and South American continents. By 1570, Spanish explorers had found the potato-rich area of modern Bolivia/Peru. These explorers had never seen a potato before, so they gathered some to take back to show the king and queen what they had found. The king and queen tried and loved the potato, and for a brief period, it was the food of the wealthy.

Potatoes, though, quickly became commonplace on all European tables. The English had also stumbled upon the potato in the New World and were importing potatoes by 1588. Not only were potatoes being imported, but they were also being grown on European soil. Although the potato was not native to Europe, it grew well in Europe's soil. It grew so well that leaders encouraged the peasants to plant them. The potato had a great taste; it didn't spoil quickly, it was filling, and it was cheap.

It didn't hurt that a prominent nun and Spanish church reformer, Saint Teresa of Avila, had cooked the potato the way people of the Mediterranean cooked vegetables. Teresa had cut it into thin strips and fried it, a cooking method the Mayans had never used. The Belgians particularly liked her potato strips recipe, which became very popular in the region where Belgium borders France. When Americans tasted the potato treat while participating in World War I, they associated it with the French. Because many Americans tried it and liked it in Europe, American restaurants began offering it after the war. When the American company J.R. Simplot discovered the ability to safely freeze potato strips in the late 1940s, restaurants no longer had to peel their own potatoes. In the 1950s, fast food establishments like McDonald's were pushing the low cost-high profit product, and by the 1960s, shoppers could purchase frozen potato strips from the grocery store.

The fried potato strip has many names worldwide and comes in over thirty different shapes and sizes. Some are thick, and some are narrow; some are curly, and some are straight; some are round, and some are rectangular. In Great Britain, they are known as "chips"; in France, they are called "frites"; but here in the United States, potato strips are known as . . . **French fries.**

FUN FACTS

When a fast-food employee asks, "Do you want fries with that?" the employee is using a marketing technique called "suggestive selling."

U.S. President Thomas Jefferson is thought to have acquainted Americans with French fries; he brought some back from an 1802 trip to France.

The French fry is the national dish of Belgium.

CHAPTER 15

Free Food – and It was Good

In the food and beverage industry, reputation is essential. If you have a good product but a bad reputation, no one will buy it. In 1960, squid had a big image problem. Squid may have been a Mediterranean food for thousands of years, but in North America, squid was not considered food. Squid was considered so worthless it was used as bait, and if fishermen caught more squid than they needed for bait by chance, they just threw the rest back into the ocean.

Helen Randazzo, Randazzo's Clam Bar owner in Sheepheads Bay in Brooklyn, New York, wished her customers liked squid. Not only was squid a low-cost and high-profit item in the 1970s and 1980s, but cod and other fish that Randazzo usually sold were also in short supply. The ocean had been overfished, and fish had not reproduced enough to meet the demand. A short supply meant higher prices, fewer sales, and/or smaller profits. If only her clientele would eat squid, she thought.

Helen realized squid had just an image problem; once people tasted it, they liked it. She realized people were repulsed by the thought of eating "squid", so on her menu, she listed squid as "calamari," the Italian word for squid. She believed that "calamari" sounded exotic. Most people didn't know what calamari was, but in their minds, it did not produce the image of a "squid," so they were more willing to taste it.

To further entice her customers to try it, she offered it fresh from the deep fryer for free. Who is going to turn down free food? The squid cost her almost nothing and brought patrons into the bar.

Ever heard the slogan, "There ain't no free lunch?" The patrons might have thought this was a free meal, for Helen gave away free calamari and dipping sauces. Helen's profits rose substantially, though. She served spicy sauces, and patrons needed to drink to put out the chili fire. The fried squid and the sauces were free, but the beverages were not.

When other restaurants saw that Helen was doing well, they, too, started to serve calamari, driving up the cost. Before long, the price had gone so high that calamari was the food of only the rich in the Boston and New York area; quite an ironic twist when you realize that people wouldn't even try squid a few months before. Eventually, fishermen caught up to the demand, and the middle class could also afford to eat squid. Today, squid is still offered as an appetizer in many middle-class restaurants. As you might suspect, nobody calls it "squid from the deep fryer"; instead, it is known as . . . **fried calamari.**

FUN FACTS

Squids range in size from one inch to over 80 feet, but most are about a foot long.

"Calamari" and "squid" are the same thing; the "octopus" is the squid's cousin.

Many restaurants do not serve the tentacles to make squids seem less grotesque.

CHAPTER 16
The Bartering Bean That Became a Brewed Beverage

In primitive societies, everyone was a hunter and gatherer, and everyone in a clan would participate in foraging for food. As people stopped being nomads and began farming, specializations began to appear. One person would need to trade what they had produced to another person for what the other person had produced. Money was not yet invented, so people would have to barter. A person could ask whatever they wanted for an item, and if someone accepted the price, the trade was made. It wasn't long, though, before exchange rates had been formalized, and people began to understand the value of what they had. For instance, 30 cocoa beans could buy a turkey in ancient Mexico. The cocoa beans could then be used to barter for something else, or one could crush them, creating cocoa or chocolate. (Although we tend to use the words "cocoa" and "chocolate" interchangeably, "cocoa" refers to the powdered bean with the cocoa butter removed, and "chocolate" refers to the processed bar which has both cocoa butter and sugar.)

In 1900 BCE, people of the Olec Empire, the predecessor of the Maya and Aztec Empires, had learned how to melt cocoa. They would turn the cocoa into a paste with water, cornmeal, and chili peppers and then mix the drink by pouring it from a pot into a cup and back into the pot. When it was mixed, they would let it cool and then drink it. They had no sugar, so the drink was very bitter and spicy.

The Maya and Aztecs continued the tradition of drinking melted cocoa. The Maya Empire flourished in the cocoa area, and people of all classes enjoyed the cold beverage throughout the empire. Meanwhile, cocoa beans could not be grown in the climate of the Aztec Empire, but the Aztecs imported cocoa, and they, too, drank the cold, spicy, bitter cocoa beverage. Although loved by Central and South Americans, cold cocoa reminded a secret from the rest of the world until the 1500s when European and South American cultures collided with Spanish explorers coming upon Mayan and Aztec villages.

Chocolate was unheard of in Europe, and the cold cocoa drink was a taste they had never experienced until the Spanish explorer Cortez took chocolate back to Spain and shared the drink recipe with the court of King Charles V. The Spanish court welcomed it but kept it a secret from all other nations for almost 100 years. The Spanish court gradually made a couple of changes to the recipe, though; they did away with the chili peppers and started serving it hot.

Not only did the Spaniards' hot drink taste great, but it was also thought to have medicinal powers, such as being good for the stomach, reducing fever, and healing liver disease. Modern scientists at Cornell University have not found research to support that, but they have proven that the drink helps prevent heart disease. The drink has become increasingly popular in the United States and can be found in many vending machines. If you want to try some, go to a coffee vending machine and press . . . **hot chocolate.**

FUN FACTS

The first chocolate candy bar was not sold until 1876; the solid form of chocolate is more popular than the liquid form today.

In the 1700s, cocoa powder was invented in Holland; the powder mixed more easily with milk and water than cocoa beans.

Hot chocolate served cold was so valued by the Mayans that the rich often buried their chocolate-making pot with them so they could have it in the next world.

CHAPTER 17
The Past Met the Present and Created a Bright Future. Oh Yeah!

Have you ever been walking along and suddenly thought of something from your past? For instance, I hadn't thought about my grandma's homemade cherry pies for years, but the other day a smell in the air brought the memory back to me. Psychologists say the normal brain never forgets; it may misfile things, but all that information is still in there and can be retrieved under the right conditions.

Edwin Perkins had a flashback in 1927. When he was eleven in 1900, his family sold their farm and moved to a nearby town where his dad opened a general store. Edwin helped at the store, spinning penny-candy displays for customers and making product recommendations. He was particularly fond of the store's new product, Jell-o, and urged his dad to keep all six flavors in stock.

Edwin enjoyed the day-to-day activities of the general store. He listened to people's needs and realized the store didn't have all the products to meet them. However, he enjoyed chemistry and believed he could make products to help meet people's needs. His family encouraged him, his dad letting him work at the store, and his mom letting him tinker with chemicals in the kitchen. He made perfumes, soft drinks, and a mixture designed to cause people to stop smoking. The store patrons were receptive to his work; he also started a mail-order business to enhance his sales.

One of his best-selling products was a beverage he called Fruit Smack. Fruit Smack was a concentrate; customers had to add water, saving shipping costs tremendously. Even so, shipping was a nightmare. The glass jars Fruit Smack came in, though, often got broken in shipment and were expensive to send. Overall, he was reduced to selling Fruit Smack door to door in his rural Nebraska community.

One day, he suddenly remembered the powdered Jell-o he had seen as a youth. Somehow, he reasoned, there should be a way to remove the liquid from Fruit Smack, leaving just a powdery residue, crystals that, when mixed with water, would come back to life. He kept experimenting and, in 1927, found how to do it, creating a base for fruit drinks and fruit-flavored desserts. He didn't do it for just one flavor; he did it for six – cherry, grape, lemon-lime, orange, raspberry, and strawberry, just as Jell-o had done. He then designed the packaging; he started with envelopes and later added tubs.

A couple of years later, though, Edwin had a problem. His powdered drink mix was a luxury enjoyed by children, and with the onset of the Great Depression, most people could not afford the dime he asked. Edwin had a kind heart and knew that selling lots of units at a lower price was more profitable than selling a few at a high price, so he dropped the price to a nickel.

In 1953 he sold his company to General Foods, the same company that made Jell-o. General Foods made some significant branding changes. It added lemonade and root beer flavors. It then asked Marvin Potts to create a brand mascot. Marvin created Pitcher Man, a cartoon pitcher placed on the envelopes; General Foods also added the slogan, "A five-cent package makes two quarts." Edwin passed away in 1961, so he never saw the mascot General Foods introduced in 1974, a six-foot humanoid pitcher full of cherry Kool-Aid that burst through walls to assist thirsty people. The pitcher became a cultural icon. Children in the ad would say, "Hey, Kool-Aid Man," and the pitcher would reply, "Oh yeah!"

You're likely wondering why they called the mascot "Kool-Aid Man," especially since when Edwin sold his first powdered envelope in 1927, he called his flavor crystals "Kool-ade." It's because, in 1934, he changed the name of the product to what it is today **. . . Kool-Aid.**

FUN FACTS

Kool-Aid is the official soft drink of Nebraska, where Edwin invented it.

In 1983, Kool-Aid Man became a comic book character. There have been seven *The Adventures of Kool-Aid Man* since then, produced by Marvel Comics and Archie Comics.

Kool-Aid stains and people have used it to dye everything from Easter eggs to human hair.

Pitcher Man, the forerunner of Kool-Aid Man, was inspired by a child's drawing of a smiley face in condensation on a cold window.

CHAPTER 18
The State Secret That Became Common Knowledge

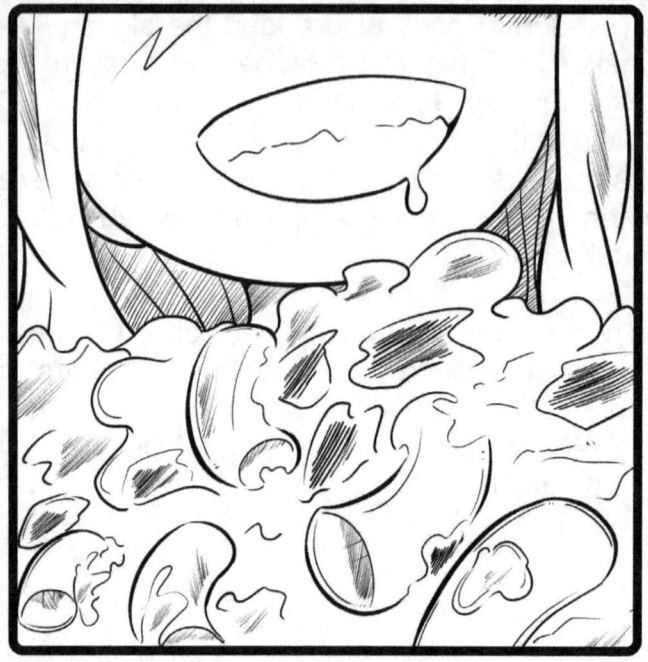

Marcus Cato was a Roman Senator in 160 B.C.E. He strongly opposed Roman society incorporating Greek societal ways into it. He had grown up with Roman ways and wanted to retain Roman culture, even if the rest of the known world was adapting to Greek influence. He knew that he and his ultraconservative friends had a lot of work to do to make converts of other senators, so he sat down and wrote a book, *De Agri Cultura*, on how the government should be run and how to influence people to run it that way.

One of his beliefs was that one needed food for a good dialog. Having shared this belief in the front of the book, in the back of the book, he provided recipes for making such food. One of the recipes showed how macaroni pasta, and cheese could be combined. Scholars aren't certain if this was a recipe Cato had developed or if he merely shared what was already popular in culture; they do know that this is the first reference to cheese and macaroni pasta.

In 1789, France followed Cato's advice and served a hot cheese and macaroni pasta dish to U.S. diplomat Thomas Jefferson, who would become the third President of the United States. Jefferson was so impressed that he brought the recipe back to the United States and shared the dish. Cheese combined with macaroni pasta was not unheard of in the United States, but with Jefferson's influence, it gained great acceptance.

Although it had been the feasts of Roman senators and U.S. Presidents during the Great Depression, cheese and macaroni pasta became popular with the working-class diet. Cheese combined with macaroni pasta was not only healthy, but it was also filling and very economical. Whereas macaroni pasta at one time was expensive, thanks to new technology, macaroni pasta could be mass-produced.

Healthy, filling, and economical were great selling points, but Canadian cheesemaker J. L. Kraft added a fourth – convenience, making it a staple for busy parents, struggling college students, and the poor. Kraft provided a kit with macaroni, cheese, and easy-to-follow directions. Although this cheesy dish of macaroni noodles goes by a variety of names, such as Mac and Cheese, Macaroni Cheese, Macaroni Pie, most people know it as . . . **Macaroni and Cheese.**

FUN FACTS

Although many copied President Jefferson in incorporating macaroni and cheese into their lives in the early 1800s, macaroni, and cheese was already well established as a food of celebration among African-Americans.

Kraft Macaroni and Cheese has not always come in a blue box. When it was introduced in 1934, it was in a yellow box. The blue box premiered in 1954.

For many people, Macaroni and Cheese is a comfort food. (A comfort food is a food that one looks at with nostalgia and sentimentality.)

Kraft Macaroni and Cheese introduced the world to something it had never seen – powdered cheese.

CHAPTER 19
Gimmicks and Good Taste

Do you have a smartphone or a similar "smart" device? Sometimes I wonder how smart those devices are because the manufacturer pushes out a software update every few weeks. The phone may have been smart before, but it is smarter now. Ironically, what is top of the line today will be outdated in a few weeks.

Charles Elmer Hires could relate to that feeling, even though he lived in the 1880s long before the invention of cell phones. Charles was a pharmacist, and pharmacists were always experimenting. They would combine this plant with that plant, this root with that root, and then see what resulted. Sassafras, for instance, had been a medicine used by Native Americans for years, but now different roots were being combined with it, creating new medicines and tastes.

Charles carefully recorded each of his experiments, noting which roots he used, how much of them, and how much water he added. In 1875, Charles developed a tea made from sassafras. Charles knew he had a good product, a wonderful drink, but he had a slight problem – how would he convince people to drink his product? Charles had a couple of ideas.

In 1876, Charles sold his beverage to thirsty fair attendees at the Philadelphia Centennial Exposition, an extravaganza that celebrated the 100th birthday of the United States, and it gained nationwide notice. By 1886 he was successfully bottling it; by 1893, it was readily available around the United States.

Charles was not the first nor the last to make a sassafras beverage – or a beverage from other roots; some recipes date back to colonial America in the 1600s. These early recipes, though, were generally cold remedies for one person, not a refreshing drink for the masses. Charles realized that the concept of "root tea" – what his invention was - would not fare well among the Pennsylvania miners he desired to sell his product to if he called it Root Tea, so he had a second marketing brainstorm. Although he was a teetotaler, he decided to give the product a macho image by calling it . . . **root beer.**

FUN FACTS

Sassafras was one of the first things European explorers took back from North America.

Sassafras comprises most root beers but not all; Barq's, for instance, is sarsaparilla-based.

Roy Allen, the founder of A&W root beer, developed a marketing gimmick that worked – he sold his root beer in chilled, frosty mugs.

Because of all the various combinations of roots and herbs that can be used to make root beer, most root beer brands have a distinctive flavor.

CHAPTER 20

The Delicious Product Nobody Wanted to Buy

Do you like French fries? I do.

French Fries are long straight pieces of potato that have been fried in oil and then usually salted. If you know anything about potatoes, you know they are oval. Therefore, some potato parts will be too small to make a French fry that meets a manufacturer's self-imposed benchmark. This means that there will be waste from each potato.

Nephi Grigg realized this the hard way. In the late 1940s, Nephi talked his brother Golden into mortgaging their farms and pooling that money with their life's savings to buy a foreclosed food processing plant near where Idaho and Oregon intersect with Ontario, Canada. The brothers had been farmers in the Great Depression during World War Two, raising potatoes, corn, and dairy cattle. The food processing plant had specialized in frozen corn but had gone out of business; Nephi was willing to continue to have the plant produce frozen corn, but his long-term goal was to specialize in frozen potatoes.

The technology to create the French fry was developed in 1946; it is covered elsewhere in this book. Nephi believed that French fries would be a staple of the American diet, and he was willing to put all his money behind his idea. His frozen fries sold extremely well, and his plant, which he had named Ore-Ida since it was located on the Oregon-Idaho border, acquired a large chunk of the very profitable frozen food market. Nephi, though, saw the waste created by the small potatoes, scrap pieces, and gunk that formed on the cutting blades.

One day one of the machines needed repair. A repairman was called, and he got the machine working again. While he worked, he visited with Nephi and described how a prune-sorting machine could be adjusted to sort the good potatoes from the potato waste. Nephi purchased one, bagged all the potato scraps, and sold them as cattle feed.

Using the waste potatoes as cattle food was being a good steward of the product, and the proceeds were better than nothing. Still, Nephi believed a more financially profitable option had to exist. Noticing how the scraps clumped together, he made fried potato clumps. He took a glob, put flour on it, and then fried it. He realized he could get the clumps in a uniform shape by pushing the dough-like raw potatoes through a cylinder, making them all the same size. He experimented with different batter recipes until he found one that he preferred. What caused him to rebrand his idea was when he realized that they tasted just as good baked as they did fried.

Convinced he had a great product, in 1954, he went to the chef at the Miami hotel hosting the National Potato Convention. He offered to give the chef 15 pounds of his battered potato clumps to serve to the breakfasting conventioneers. The chef accepted the product – and a bribe– and served the newly created potato product to the potato connoisseurs as part of their breakfast. The product was a hit at the convention.

In 1956, the product was released to the American public – and no one was interested in buying it. Sales were dismal. Nephi was dumbfounded. He knew he had a product that people liked when they tried it. He knew the price was low. He couldn't deny, though, that people would look at his product and keep on walking.

Upon reflection, he realized what the problem was. Potato scraps were now perceived as cattle food and virtually worthless – which they were. Nephi had priced his product very low to pass the savings on to the consumer, confirming the customer's perception that the product was worthless. Nephi raised the price, pricing the potato clumps for humans far above the costs of potato clumps for animals but still affordable to middle-class families.

Nephi displayed marketing genius when he got the conventioneers to become excited about the product and again when he enhanced the product's image by raising its price, but the staying power of the product was using alliteration – the use of the same consonant sound in two or more consecutive words - when naming the product. The potato pieces may never have been popular if they were called "baked potato clumps" or "French fry rejects", but they won the heart of children and adults alike with the name . . . **Tater Tots.**

FUN FACTS

Nephi enjoyed revising slogans that were popular in culture. For instance, you have probably been told, "Don't bite off more than you can chew" – an idiom that applies to table food but to life as well; he said, "Bite off more than you can chew. Then chew it."

"Tater" is short for "potato."

Other vegetables have also become tots. Today, you can purchase "cauliflower tots" and "broccoli tots."

Tater Tots is still a trademarked name, but the term is often used to describe any brand's fried potato chunk.

CHAPTER 21

So Simple It's Grand

Imagine that you are the maître d'hotel for the Waldorf Hotel (later the Waldorf-Astoria Hotel) in New York City in 1893. The hotel had just opened the day before, and tonight is the hotel's first big event – a charity gala to raise money for a children's hospital. Over 1,500 people from upper-class society will be coming from New York, Boston, Philadelphia, and Baltimore to the hotel. The head chef has planned a generic menu, saying he wants a salad. What kind of salad would you serve? What kind of salad would be bold and classy, exotic but tame, tasty, and memorable?

Oscar Tschirky, a Swiss restaurateur, held the maître d'hotel position, and he faced that exact question. The hotel's reputation depended on what he did; the success of the fundraiser depended on what he did; more importantly, to him, his job depended on what he did. Whereas you and I can answer the question hypothetically, Oscar had to provide the final answer.

Oscar's answer was to keep it simple – to offer a salad consisting only of apples, celery, and lettuce. Perhaps it was the beauty of the greens side by side; perhaps it was the simplicity. Whatever it was, people loved it!

The recipe was simple, so it spread quickly. The salad could be an appetizer or even a light meal. People added an ingredient here and there to suit their tastes; in particular, sliced grapes and chopped walnuts were common additions in the early twentieth century. Mayonnaise, oranges, and marshmallows were also common as the twentieth century pulled to a close.

Oscar didn't want people to forget the original three-ingredient recipe. Within three years, he had done so many signature dishes at the Waldorf that he had a reputation around all of New York; that reputation was so great that he published and sold a cookbook, *The Cook Book by Oscar of the Waldorf.*

If you thought Oscar kept his salad ingredients simple and his book title equally simple, then you'll not be surprised to know that he kept the name of his salad simple as well; he called it . . . **the Waldorf Salad.**

FUN FACTS

A Waldorf Salad can be made in under ten minutes.

Besides the Waldorf Salad, Oscar created Lobster Newburg and Veal Oscar.

When Oscar passed away in 1950, the Philanthropique Society purchased his farm and turned it into a retirement home for chefs.

PART THREE:
ENTREES

CHAPTER 22

A Taste Worth Going Out of the Way For

When traveling down the highway, don't you love to see the signs that read "Road Construction Next Twenty Miles"? (I'm being facetious.) That usually means there will be lots of slow traffic, roads going down to one lane, orange barrels sitting on the roadside, bright lights, concrete barriers on the road's shoulder, construction noises, and closed exits.

You may despise road construction as a driver, but you must pity those whose businesses depend upon the traffic going up and down the road. If the road construction will last a long time – and some road projects are years, this can significantly impact a business's profits.

In 1961, road construction began on I-96 in Lansing, Michigan. For those unfamiliar with Michigan geography, I-96 runs between Detroit and Grand Rapids. Dave Mulder, the owner of a franchise A&W drive-in, was one of the merchants cut off from the interstate. A&W was known for its root beer, but the lure of root beer alone would not get people to travel many miles out of their way to come to his restaurant.

In 1963, with road construction on the interstate still far from being completed, Dave pondered what to do. His employees depended on him to stay open for their livelihoods, and the town loved his restaurant, but he was not making it financially without the interstate traffic. As he pondered, he ate a cheeseburger, and at that moment, inspiration struck. "I bet it would taste even better with bacon," Dave mused.

Dave decided to try it with bacon to see if he was right. In his opinion, it did taste better with bacon. Dave began to wonder if other people would agree with him. Although Dave was part of the A&W chain, local restaurants could choose their own menus provided they served A&W brand root beer. Deciding it wouldn't hurt to find out if people would enjoy bacon on cheeseburgers, Dave began advertising and selling his bacon and cheeseburger at his restaurant. No one else at that time was selling them, so if someone wanted a hot, gooey cheeseburger with bacon, they had to come to his restaurant – and that, with his A&W root beer, was enough to inspire people to drive miles out of their way.

The cheeseburger with bacon became such a hit that other restaurants soon copied it, and cheeseburgers with bacon are now on the menu of most fast-food restaurants. Dave could have called his creation "Dave's Burger" or "The Big Dave" after himself, or he could have named it the "A&W Cheeseburger Special" or the "Cheeseburger with Bacon," but Dave decided on the name that has become a household term, the . . . **bacon cheeseburger.**

FUN FACTS

A&W is named after its founders, Roy Allen, the creator of A&W root beer, and Frank Wright, who oversaw the restaurants.

Bacon Double Cheeseburger is a real man's name. (Yes, you can legally change your name to be just about anything you want it to be.)

Although the exact order and combination of ingredients vary when constructing a bacon cheeseburger, putting the cheese and the bacon on top of the hamburger patty is tradition.

The veggie burger at Burger King has more calories than its double bacon cheeseburger.

CHAPTER 23
Donkey Ears

Juan Mendez owned a taco stand in the Bella Vista neighborhood of Juarez, Mexico, during the turbulent years of the Mexican Revolution, 1910 – 1921. Times were difficult, but he was able to eke out a living. Each day he would take his supplies by donkey from his home to his taco stand, and each evening he and his donkey would return home to prepare to cook for the next day.

Juan had a major problem. He lived so far away from his taco stand that his food was cold when he got there. Unfortunately for Juan, there was not a great market for cold tacos. Juan knew that if he wanted to stay in business, he had to find a way to keep his ingredients warm. He thought and came up with four choices. Option one, he could make his burro (donkey) go faster, but it was going as fast as it could, so that option wasn't realistic. Option two, he could move the taco stand, but it was in an affluent neighborhood with great potential for high sales, so this option wasn't realistic either. Option three, he could move closer to the taco stand. The times were tough, though; financially, that was not a realistic option. That left option four. Option four was to find a way to insulate the food better to stay warmer longer.

Finding a way to insulate the food better was by far the more realistic option. He decided to wrap the warm tortilla shells, the hot meat, and the refried beans in a tablecloth and then put them in saddlebags on his small donkey. The idea helped, but he lived so far away that the food was still not pleasantly warm when prospective patrons came to his booth.

Juan then had another idea for keeping the food warm. He decided to wrap the taco in tortilla shells, believing that the shell would further insulate the ingredients. He measured cheese, meat, sauce, and beans for each tortilla shell and then sold the shell as a unit. His taco rolls were hot, fresh, tasty, and twice the length of a typical taco. He had a hit on his hands.

Juan's invention might have tasted like a taco – after all, numerous types of meats, sauces, and vegetables could be placed in the tortilla, just as they could on a taco - but they sure didn't look like a taco. People didn't take long to devise a name for Juan's unique tacos.

Today, everybody agrees on the name for the rolled taco, but exactly how people came up with the name is debated (and a few people even argue that it wasn't even Juan who came up with the idea of the rolled taco). They all agreed that Juan's creation should be called "little donkey." Many people say that it is because Juan carried the taco rolls on his donkey and that they chose the name in honor of his donkey. Others claim that it is because the taco rolls looked like donkey ears. Some say it is because the rolled tacos looked like the blankets small donkeys often carried. They all agreed that Juan's taco rolls should be called "little donkeys." Of course, his patrons were Spanish speakers, so they used the Spanish words for "little donkey"; therefore, you and I call this rolled taco the **. . . burrito.**

FUN FACTS

Although it wasn't called a burrito, wrapping one's food in a corn tortilla can be traced back to the Mayan culture of the 1500s.

Before burritos became a name for food, being called a "burrito" was an insult children would call to one another; the English children had a similar expression, "donkey face."

Although people think of burritos as Mexican food, they are only popular in northern Mexico but not in southern Mexico. The main reason is that wheat, a primary ingredient in the burrito shell, cannot be grown in southern Mexico.

CHAPTER 24

Reverse Sushi

Have you ever tried to get a dog or a kid to take a pill? If you have, you know that if they know that you want them to take a pill, they will likely back away from you. If you pretend you ate one, they still refuse it. If you suggest they "open the hangar to let the airplane in" and then try to put the pill in their mouth, they will grit their teeth in defiance. If you push it toward their mouth, they will turn their head. Therefore, many people hide the pill in their food where they will consume it and not even realize that they have ingested it.

Japanese chef Hidekazu Tojo migrated to Canada in 1971 and opened a restaurant. Although Japanese citizens had been migrating to Canada for years, and sushi had become a dish in Japanese restaurants in Canada since the early 1800s, sushi did not enjoy wide appeal. Tojo wanted to introduce his new friends to some of his favorite Japanese dishes, particularly sushi, a Japanese dish made of rice, cucumber, ginger, and crab meat or raw fish since at least 400 CE. However, eating raw seaweed repulsed his customers, who wanted nothing to do with it.

Tojo was convinced they would like seaweed if they tried it; they had tried raw fish and liked it. One day, he had an idea – instead of wrapping the rice and meat in a seaweed wrapper, he would wrap the seaweed and meat in rice. He took strips of avocado, spinach, boiled crab, egg omelet, and seafood in a rice roll. He named the creation after himself; he called the roll the Tojo Roll. His customers did not realize they were eating seaweed, so they accepted the dish. The dish became so popular that "reverse sushi" became a North American dish that became a reverse import, making its way to Japan.

The supply of seafood ebbs and flows. When crab was in short supply, Tojo replaced the crabmeat in the Tojo Roll with imitation crab. (Imitation crab is white fish with fillers that mimic crab's texture and taste.) The imitation crab appealed to his clientele even more than the pure crab meat did, and the recipe spread down the West Coast, particularly taking root in southern California and the city of Los Angeles. By the 1990s, the modified Tojo Roll was a tasty dish popular throughout the United States. When he replaced the crab meat with artificial crab, Tojo distinguished it with a different name. Since the treat had avocado in it and avocado came from California, Tojo called the creation . . . **the California Roll.**

FUN FACTS

Traditional Japanese sushi usually contains raw seafood, particularly eel, squid, salmon, tuna, and crab.

Because he called it the California roll, many people assumed the invention came from California instead of Canada, just like they assume French fries originated in France. Although many chefs in Los Angeles have claimed to be the inventor of the California roll, Tojo is generally accepted as its inventor.

Since the California roll uses imitation cráb and does not have seaweed on the outside, some food critics do not regard the California roll as sushi.

CHAPTER 25
Supper? Breakfast? You Decide

Dickie Wells was a light-skinned African American tap dancer at the Cotton Club in Harlem during the Harlem Renaissance. To say he was a tap dancer is putting it mildly; he was a fantastic tap dancer. Dickie, though, knew that he was not always going to be a fantastic dancer; he knew that his youthfulness would fade and he would become just one of many. In 1929, he was 21 and could already feel himself slipping.

Dickie loved the theater and wanted to keep being a part of it. Therefore, in the early 1930s, he opened a nightclub that catered to musicians after all the other clubs in the area closed. Many performers were still on adrenaline from their performance, and sleep was not an option for them; he gave them a place where they were welcome to hang out.

He attracted the best of the best. Although he catered to African American clientele, all races were welcome, and Clark Gable and Charlie Chaplin hung out just like Cab Calloway, Ethel Waters, and Duke Ellington. In addition to being a hangout, he also provided live entertainment; many musicians wanted to keep playing even after the show was over.

One of Dickie's predicaments was determining a menu. He had a clientele most restaurants could only dream of and wanted to keep them returning. He was torn between a traditional supper menu and a traditional breakfast menu. The hours of three, four, and five a.m. are not exactly supper hours, but they aren't breakfast either. He finally decided to offer a combination of supper and breakfast – literally. He took fried chicken and placed it on a plate with waffles. The customer could decide between bourbon and coffee to go with it; if one chose bourbon, it was a supper dish; if one chose coffee, it was a breakfast dish.

Putting chicken and waffles together was nothing new; the Pennsylvania Dutch had done it in the 1600s but used baked chicken. Putting fried chicken and waffles together was a soulful twist on an old favorite. He could have chosen any name he wanted, but he decided to call the dish **. . . Chicken and Waffles.**

FUN FACTS

Cornelius Swartwout invented the modern waffle iron in 1869.

The word "waffle" is from the Frankish word for "honeycomb" or "cake."

The instrumental jazz piece "Chicken and Waffles" was composed in 1935.

The ancient Greeks are credited with inventing the waffle; they enjoyed eating cakes made by pressing two hot metal plates together.

The term "a.m.", as in "3 a.m." means "ante meridiem," before noon. P.M., meanwhile, means "post meridiem," after noon.

CHAPTER 26
The Evolution of the Hotdog

Many of our favorite foods were neither accidental inventions nor the result of a chef's brainstorm; these foods were a gradual evolution, with one idea for improvement being placed on top of a previous idea. For instance, let's follow the history of the hotdog.

The hotdog has its roots in sausage. As described elsewhere in this book, sausage was the first processed food. It consisted of a lamb's intestine being stuffed with meat scraps. Over time, these packs of meat scraps specialized, becoming baloney, salami, and, in 1497, the hotdog.

Two cities vie for the title of the birthplace of the hotdog, Frankfurt, Germany, and Vienna, Austria. Sometimes you will hear the hotdog referred to as a "frank" or a "frankfurter," a tip of the hat to Frankfurt, Germany. Other times you will hear the hotdog called the "wiener," a tip of the hat to Vienna, Austria, which the Germans pronounce as "Wien."

In the 1860s, the hotdog found its way into the American diet. German immigrants settling into the United States spread the gospel of the hotdog from vending carts on street corners. The pork sausage looked like a dash and reminded people of the dachshund. The sausage was served hot, so by 1900, the "frankfurter," "frank," and "wiener" became best known as the "hotdog."

In the 1920s, the hotdog had an image problem in the United States. The United States had just finished fighting Germany in World War I, and anything German was still suspect - as was anyone associated with it. Wanting to be perceived as patriotic, most Americans avoided German food. Calling it the "hotdog" rather than German-rooted words such as "frankfurter" and "wiener" helped but did not solve the problem.

Sausage vendors in Texas were not immune from this stigma. In the early 1920s, a butcher shop in Texas decided to deep fry the German sausage in cornmeal; people who tried it initially did not know what they were eating. Before they could find out what it was, they had fallen in love with it and were willing to overlook that it was a German invention. By 1926, catalogs contained machines people could use to deep-fry the hotdogs; not only were the hotdogs cooked in cornmeal, but the machines also resulted in the dough having a corn-on-the-cob appearance.

In 1927, an impale-your-food-with-a-wooden-stick fad swept the nation. Impaling one's food allowed one to eat it without using utensils or fingers. People impaled food ranging from strawberries to eggs. Naturally, someone – or several someones, it is possible many people tried it independently of each other - decided to impale the breaded hotdog. Stanley Jenkins, though, is the person who submitted the patent; it was approved by the U.S. government in 1929.

In 1938, Carl and Neil Fletcher introduced the food to the world at the Texas State Fair; since then, it has become a fair food staple. Carl and Neil called the food "Corny Dog", and others have called it "Korn Dog," "Corn Dog," and "Hotdog on a Stick," but most people know this treat as the . . . **Corndog.**

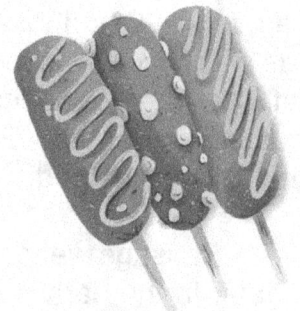

FUN FACTS

Corndogs may be tasty, but they have almost no nutritional value.

A typical corndog is 330 calories.

Before corndogs were put on sticks, people ate the breaded hotdog using various methods; using wax paper as a napkin to hold it, using their fingers, holding it in a paper cone, and even stabbing it with a pocketknife.

CHAPTER 27

Fit for a King but Served in the Slum

1845 to 1852 were terrible years to be an Irish citizen in Ireland. The potato famine had wiped out most of the food supply and would not let the growing resume. Over one million people would die from famine in those years; over one million more had to move. Moving or starving were the only options for most people. Many of those affected by the famine moved to the United States.

1845 to 1852 were terrible years to be an Irish person in the United States. Although the United States was largely composed of former immigrants, many of these people had been settled in the young nation for several generations. They did not appreciate the competition for their jobs, the disease, and the crime that the Irish brought. America was prejudiced, and they did not welcome the Irish openly.

However, America's borders were open, and many Irish – legally and illegally - settled in large cities such as New York and Boston. Irish neighborhoods – slums, to be less euphonical - sprung up in these cities. In their neighborhoods, the Irish often interacted with people from other self-segregated neighborhoods, such as the Jews and Italians. Jews, for instance, would come through with carts of meat from which the Irish would purchase.

One of the meats that Jews carried was corned beef. Corned beef had nothing to do with corn, the vegetable; it was a brisket cured by salt the size of corn kernels. The corned beef reminded the Irish of the Irish bacon from their homeland. The typical Irish person in the slum had grown up poor and had never eaten corned beef; it was the food of kings and landlords. In Ireland, cows had been used for plowing and milking, and they had only been eaten on rare occasions such as an injury or old age. The more cows a farmer had, the wealthier the farmer was perceived to be. So keeping cows alive led to increased social status. Also, cattle were sacred in Irish mythology, contributing to cattle seldom. If Irish farmers raised any animal to eat, it was the pig.

In the United States, though, beef was plentiful, and it was cheap enough to be affordable even to the poor. The Irish cooked corned beef with cabbage in the same pot to save money. Although not native to Ireland, the resulting dish became an Irish classic.

America grew to accept the Irish and their foods. Every March 17, everyone in the United States celebrates St. Patrick's Day, honoring the Irish heritage. On St. Patrick's Day -and for many on New Year's Day as well - it is traditional for U.S. citizens, regardless of whether they have an Irish heritage, to enjoy the Irish dish the Irish Americans created using cabbage and corned beef, a dish rarely served in Ireland but very popular among Irish in the United States . . . **corned beef and cabbage.**

The journey from Ireland to the United States lasted at least four weeks and covered over 3,000 miles.

Corned Beef and Cabbage is not the only Irish American tradition not found in Ireland. In the United States, you will find Irish with green beer and leprechauns that are friendly; in Ireland, beer is not green, and leprechauns are considered evil and nasty.

Cabbage is a great source of fiber, Vitamin C, and Vitamin K.

CHAPTER 28

The Food Known to Only Families of Butchers and Cowboys for Almost 40 Years

Do you get unique perks for working with your company that are supposed to supplement your pay? In addition to a monetary wage, some companies will pay for your insurance, some will provide a private lake house, and some will give you a company car.

In the 1930s, during the Great Depression and beyond, ranchers in the Rio Grande Valley along the southwestern Texas-Mexican border would pay their working hands a wage and give them parts of butchered cattle. These weren't prime parts; they were the heads, hides, entrails, and meat trimmings. The work hands then turned these items into dishes, though, such as head barbeque (barbacoa de cabeza), tripe stew (Menudo), and grilled skirt steak (arracheras).

The grilled skirt steak was strips of thinly sliced meat. The cowboys would marinate the meat in lime juice, place it on a wheat flour tortilla, and add thin strips of peppers and onions. The result was delicious! However, only the cowboys, their butchers, and their families knew this wonderful food. There was not enough meat to share with friends, so the skirt steak taco remained a secret.

In 1969, a butcher who knew the skirt steak taco recipe opened a taco stand at a festival in Kyle, Texas, and served them to the public. That same year, the Round-Up Restaurant in Pharr, Texas, began serving the skirt steak as the meat of a make-your-own-taco. The word about the skirt steak taco spread slowly through southern Texas, reaching major Texas cities such as Houston and Austin. Believing urbanites would like this food treat, in 1982, the Hyatt of Austin added a skirt steak taco to its menu.

Skirt steak had been the food of the poor, rural cowboy but was now offered to a high-brow clientele. The Hyatt cooking staff presented the skirt steak to diners on a sizzling iron skillet to add pizzazz to the presentation. Like the Round-Up Restaurant, it allowed people to put their own combination of peppers, meat, and onion onto the wheat tortilla shells. Hyatt owned hotels nationwide, and what had become a regional food soon became a national food. The skirt steak taco's place in American culture was cemented in 1991 when the fast-food giant McDonald's started offering it. Although it was introduced as a beef product, when it became popular, people began substituting strips of chicken and even shrimp.

McDonald's didn't call the skirt steak product the "skirt strip taco;" they used the Latin word for "strip," "little band," and "belt." Butchers first used the word in the 1930s to describe the steak. Today most Americans call this combination of tortilla, onions, pepper, and skirt steak by this name also, the . . . **fajita.**

FUN FACTS

Fajitas are an American food, but they are based on Mexican tacos al carbon. There are some major differences between the two. Fajitas have wheat shells, and tacos al carbon have corn shells. Also, fajitas usually have multiple ingredients inside them, whereas tacos al carbon are usually just meat.

Today, almost all Mexican restaurants carry fajitas.

The soft sirloin section is often used instead of the skirt steak in modern fajitas; it is a much better cut of meat.

Skirt steak is located between a cow's heart and lungs.

CHAPTER 29

Two Foods Each Traveled 1,000s of Miles to Unite into One Nation's Comfort Food

People become refugees for a wide variety of reasons. Sometimes it is due to war, and other times to drought. In the late 1400s, the Jewish, Muslim, and atheist populations left Spain for Portugal to escape the Spanish Inquisition.

Portugal was a haven for the Jews until the Portuguese king married a Spanish queen. Then religious intolerance found in Spain also began to be practiced in Portugal. Forced again to either convert or flee, Jewish refugees fled beyond Portugal and scattered into Europe. Jews, in particular, fled to England at this time.

The Jews brought their religion with them – and their food. The Jewish religion forbade cooking on the Sabbath (Friday night through Saturday afternoon.) Therefore, they cooked food in advance to eat. One of their favorites to fix in advance was fish, particularly cod and haddock, fried in a coat of flour or Matzo meal.

By 1781, others living in England had tried their fish and loved it so much that Jewish merchants would often wander the streets selling the fish, much like ballpark vendors wander the stadium bleachers today. By 1831, fried fish shops were popping up everywhere in England. Thanks to the invention of the railroad, fresh fish was available to all of England, not just the people on the coast – and this meant the Jewish fried fish was also available across the nation.

Like fried fish, the potato too found its way to England in the 1500s, but it came from the newly found North and South American continents. Fries have a chapter devoted to them elsewhere in this book, so we won't cover their history in detail here. Fish and fries likely existed independently for over fifty years, but suffice it to say, the two eventually met. The first time the two were seen together was in 1860 in Joseph Malin's fish and chip shop in London. By 1935, over 35,000 specialty restaurants offering fried fish and fries dotted the English countryside. To this day, fried fish and fries are comfort food in England. However, the English don't call it fried fish and fries; instead of strips of potatoes, the British sometimes serve circular slices, chips, of potatoes, and therefore, the dish is known as **. . . fish and chips.**

FUN FACTS

Unlike most foods, fish and chips were never on the British ration list in either World War.

The slang term for a fish and chip shop in England is a "chippy."

England is not the only place with fish and chip shops. Canada, New Zealand, Australia, and the United States are other nations with prominent shops.

Cod and haddock are still very popular for fried fish, but numerous other fish are also fried.

CHAPTER 30
Gravity Caused Quite a Splash

Thank goodness for gravity. Without it, we might not have some of today's tasty treats.

Gravity is the invisible force that pulls two objects toward each other in a downward direction. Gravity is what holds our feet to the earth. Gravity pulls a grape back to the earth if you toss it in the air. If you recall from science class, Isaac Newton was inspired to ponder gravity when he watched an apple – the guy must have liked looking at food as much as we do – fall from a tree, and he began to wonder why it went down instead of up. We take gravity for granted, but should we go into outer space; we would find that gravity is almost nonexistent.

For a cook, gravity can be very frustrating. More than one cook has dropped a food item and had it fall to the floor, no longer fit for human consumption. Sometimes, though, gravity works to a cook's advantage. For instance, in 1918, Philippe Mathieu, owner of Philippe the Original, a restaurant in Los Angeles, had been asked to make a submarine sandwich for a police officer. He reached for a French loaf of bread to slice but dropped the French roll. He watched in horror to see where it would land. To his amazement, it didn't hit the floor; instead, it fell into a pan full of juice from a roast. To Philippe's disgust, the bread readily soaked up the roast juice like a sponge soaks up water. The police officer was a good sport and offered to accept the sandwich still, even though it was on soggy bread. Philippe put roast beef onto the sandwich and gave it to the man. The next day, the man returned with his friends, and they all requested a sandwich made just as Philippe had made the sandwich the day before, juice and all. That's when Philippe knew he had a hit.

I say that, but maybe this happened to a fireman instead of a police officer. And maybe it wasn't Philippe's restaurant but another Los Angeles restaurant. And maybe the French bread was deliberately soaked in the roast juice because the customer had sore gums. And maybe . . .

The truth is the truth about this sandwich may never be known. The above story is the most accepted but is not the only origin story out there. All the stories agree that it was in Los Angeles and that the bread was a French roll. That's important to know because many people assume the sandwich must have come from Paris when they hear the term **. . . French dip.**

FUN FACTS

Because of gravity, an object at the equator will weigh less than the same object at the North Pole.

A "French roll" is also known as a baguette. The French love their baguettes; 32 million are eaten daily in France.

"Au jus" means "in its own juice."

CHAPTER 31

Tso, How About That Chicken?

On the West Coast of the United States lies a state called Washington. Out of all fifty states, it is the only one named after a person, named after General George Washington, the first President of the United States. What is ironic is that George Washington never visited there, never slept there, and probably didn't even comprehend the land was there.

Now, you're likely wondering, does that weird fact have anything to do with food? It has quite a lot, as you'll understand in a minute. Right now, though, let's shift our attention to a different general, a Chinese general named Zuo Zongtang. Zuo lived from 1812 to 1885. He was born a peasant in Hunan but rose to fame through military victories and gradually became the second most powerful person in the Chinese empire. He defeated invading armies and led his nation through a civil war, the Taiping Rebellion, keeping the country united. He expanded China's borders through negotiation and force; for instance, he got the Russians to vacate the border city of Ili. He was instrumental in modernizing China and a real hero to his countrymen.

Peng Chang-Kuei, also known as Peng Jia, grew up in Hunan and heard about Zuo's amazing exploits. Peng wanted to be a chef, but he combined his dream with being a patriot and became a chef at the Presidential Palace. When the Chinese government was booted off the mainland by Mao's Communists to Taiwan in 1949, Peng continued to cook for the Presidential banquets.

In the mid-1950s, Peng created a dish with Hunanese flavors. In the 1970s, Peng migrated to the United States and opened a restaurant near the United Nations building in New York, where he served his famous dish. Most Americans found it too spicy, but one person, Secretary of State Henry Kissinger, fell in love with it and talked about it everywhere he went. Henry inspired people to try Peng's restaurant and to keep his clientele; Peng adjusted the spiciness of the dish to individual tastes.

Peng could have honored anybody he wanted by naming the dish after them. He could have chosen the most famous general from Hunan, but he didn't. (The most famous general to come from Hunan was Mao.) Instead, he named the dish in honor of his boyhood hero, Zuo. Just like Peng went by Peng Chang-Kuei and Peng Jia, Zuo also went by two different names, Zuo Zongtang and Tso Tsung-tang. Peng didn't call it General Zuo Zongtang's Chicken; he called it . . . . **General Tso's Chicken.**

FUN FACTS

General Tso loved pork much more than he liked chicken.

General Tso's Chicken was not invented while General Tso was alive; therefore, needless to say, General Tso never ate any General Tso's Chicken (just like George Washington never stepped on Washington State).

As a reward for General Tso's victories, The Chinese emperor declared General Tso to be the governor of Min-Zhe, an area that included Taiwan.

Taiwan's official name is The Republic of China.

CHAPTER 32
The Best Thing Since Sliced Bread

A new taste sensation formed when two food inventions met two mechanical inventions. The two food inventions, cheese and bread, went back over 4000 years and were among the first foods people learned to make. Cheese was likely discovered when somebody carelessly left milk outside in the heat too long; bread was discovered when people in Egypt added yeast to crushed grain. Cheese and bread were often used in conjunction with each other. People put cheese on their bread, treating cheese as one of many dips and spreads. Normally, the bread was room temperature, but, in some cases, particularly in the Roman Empire, the cheese was put on bread that was so warm that it would partially melt the cheese. This relationship between bread and cheese continues to this day.

In 1912, Otto Rohwedder, a Missouri jeweler who enjoyed tinkering with gears, created a machine to slice bread and then wrap the loaf. At first, people shunned his invention, believing the bread would dry out. Rohwedder showed that it would not dry out faster than an uncut loaf. The Chillicothe Bakery Company in Chillicothe, Missouri, bought the first machine; the bakery experienced such great success with sliced bread that it wasn't long until sliced bread became a nationwide fad. Today, sliced bread is still considered one of the greatest inventions ever, and you will often hear people compare new inventions to Rohwedder's creating the bread slicer; you'll hear them declaring, "That's the greatest thing since sliced bread."

The other mechanical invention in this story occurred in stages. In 1914, an American businessman and inventor, J.L. Kraft, found a way to pasteurize cheese so it would not spoil. Although he made a fortune selling his long-lasting cheese, known as American cheese, to the U.S. Amry in World War I, he kept trying to find ways to make cheese more accessible to all people. In 1950, he developed processed cheese; in 1956, he topped that, creating individually wrapped slices of processed cheese.

During the Great Depression, people had already begun combining Rohwedder and Kraft's inventions - many people treated themselves to a "cheese dream," a piece of toasted bread with cheese on top. Although it had a new name, the cheese dream was what the Romans had served two thousand years earlier.

In 1956, though, cheese became convenient, readily accessible, and portion controlled. With both cheese and bread available in a standardized form, people could order the sandwich in restaurants and be assured of consistency. People quickly fell into a pattern of putting one or two slices of cheese between two slices of bread and then toasting the buns lightly to melt the cheese, forming a sandwich loved by children and adults alike.

The new taste sensation of two cheese slices wedged between two slices of bread had various names. In Great Britain, the sandwich was called "the toasty," "the cheese toasty," or the "toasted sandwich"; in South Africa, it is known as the "snackwich"; and in Australia, it is known as the "jaffle". In the United States, the gooey cheese sandwich is known as . . . **the grilled cheese.**

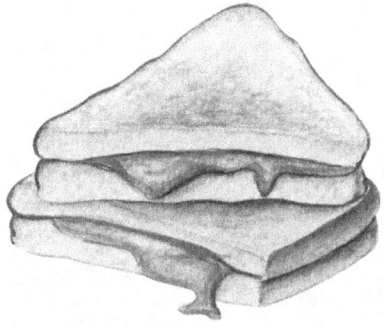

FUN FACTS

In the early 1900s, before cheese merchant James L. Kraft came along, people bought their cheese from cheese blocks and wheels cut and measured according to the customer's request. Kraft marketed his cheese differently; it came prepackaged, taking away customer choice but making speedy delivery.

As noted in the article above, in 1956, the Kraft company – J.L. Kraft retired in 1948 – invented cheese slices; in 1965, it broke new ground again, creating individually wrapped cheese slices.

Wonder Bread, owned by the Continental Baking Company, became the first nationwide sliced bread. If you have ever wondered what the two red circles, two blue circles, and one yellow circle on the Wonder logo are, wonder no more. Those represent hot air balloons, something that filled the company's vice president with wonder.

CHAPTER 33

She Turned Trash into Treasure

If you are a merchant's child, you know your parents will bring things home from the store that didn't sell to use as a family. Merchants often have a lot of money tied up in their inventory, so rather than throw away items that won't sell, the merchant will have his family use them.

Teressa Bellissimo, who co-owned the Anchor Bar in Buffalo, New York, in 1964 with her husband, had that mentality. She and her husband had acquired lots of chicken wings by mistake, and the company that sold them refused to take them back. In 1964, the Anchor Bar considered chicken wings junk parts; consumers wanted the breasts, thigh, and legs, and the consumers were not interested in eating what little meat was on the bony wing.

Around midnight, her college-aged son came into the bar with his friends. It may have been midnight, but the youth were wide awake – and hungry. They had been having a grand time and wanted to continue at the bar. Her son asked if she could make them something to eat. Realizing that the kids were expecting to eat at no charge and that rowdy teens could run up quite a tab, she pondered what she could serve. She suddenly remembered the chicken wings that were not saleable, so she decided to make them. She deep-fried them and coated them in melted butter and a vinegar-based cayenne pepper hot sauce. To offset the heat, she included sides of Blue Cheese Dressing and celery sticks when she presented them to the youth.

The youth loved them. They loved them so much that they asked for them again the next time they gathered at the bar. Soon the youths' parents were asking about these spicy wings, and, with the parents spreading the word, the whole town was asking to try them. From the town, word spread quickly through the state and then the nation. It wasn't long before her recipe was known as Buffalo Wings, named after the town where she lived. Competitors saw her success and tried to duplicate it. Although her recipe for spicy chicken was called Buffalo Wings, the competitors' wings and her wings were known by the generic term **. . . hot wings.**

FUN FACTS

Buffalos don't have wings.

Although the Anchor Bar didn't sell chicken wings in the early 1960s, fried chicken wings had been sold in Buffalo restaurants since at least 1857 when the Clarendon Hotel offered them.

Was Teressa the first to cook Buffalo Wings or simply the first to get noticed; other establishments in Buffalo claim to be the first source? Perhaps others were first, but Teressa's Anchor Bar is where they grew to nationwide fame.

Although it wasn't hot Buffalo sauce or applied by the cook, Wings 'n' Things in Washington, D.C., encouraged customers to eat wings dipped in "mumbo" sauce.

CHAPTER 34

Maybe It's Not a Jungle Out There After All

If it weren't for muckrakers, we wouldn't have the slider.

Muckraker is a term applied to American writers around the turn of the twentieth century. These writers wanted social reform, but instead of writing an essay about social reform that would bore most people, they wrote stories in which they shared issues that needed reform. One of the most famous and enduring of these books was *The Jungle* by Upton Sinclair. *The Jungle* exposed the poor conditions at the Chicago stockyards by telling the story of a Lithuanian immigrant family. The book appeared as a weekly serial in the newspaper and was bound as a novel. As a serial, it was much like a television soap opera, allowing people to follow the lives of the characters week after week. People might not have read essays or taken the time to read about a real person's plight, but they enjoyed the soap opera format of

The Jungle. As they were engrossed in the characters' adventures, they were subconsciously learning about the poor sanitation conditions of the stockyards.

The Jungle and similar works were very influential with Americans; they caused many people to stop buying beef. This hurt both the beef farmer and the restaurant industry. By 1921, beef needed an image makeover if it would continue to be a part of American culture. A restaurant owner, Walter A. Anderson, realized this and had an idea of how to do it.

First, he dressed his employees in white. Whereas the muckrakers had said that the sanitation of beef was poor, Walter wanted to show that his restaurant was clean. His counter help all wore white paper hats and white aprons.

Second, he sold his beef product cheaply. He had his cook, Edgar Ingram, who would eventually become his business partner, cook small meat patties; this allowed him to sell his burgers much cheaper than other burger places. He also adjusted the bun size; instead of being served on a hamburger bun, he sold them on dinner rolls.

Third, he created a fun atmosphere. His order takers put on a show for people, sometimes almost literally. One of the things the counter crew did was take the finished burger from Edgar and slide it down the counter on a porcelain plate to the recipient. His restaurant had an impromptu feel of zaniness.

Four, the food was tasty. These greasy, miniature hamburgers almost literally slid down one's throat; they were so good. Thanks to this miniature hamburger, beef was back in the average American's diet.

No one knows for sure where these miniature hamburgers got their name. Maybe it was because the cooks slid the burgers down the countertop, perhaps it was the ease with which they came out of their boxes, maybe it was the way Edgar moved them around the grill, or perhaps it was because the food slid down one's throat. Maybe it was all four reasons. Although the reason for the name is debatable, no one questions the name of those miniature hamburgers; they were **. . . sliders.**

FUN FACTS

"A slider with a lid" was White Castle's nickname for a cheeseburger.

Although sliders were originally hamburgers, the term has come to refer to any sandwich on a small bun; hence, there are chicken sliders.

Although "slider" became a generic term for any sandwich on a small bun, in later years, White Castle copyrighted the term "slyder." Hence, to get a genuine "slyder," one must go to White Castle.

CHAPTER 35
It's No Coincidence Unwanted Email, and Lunchmeat Share the Same Name

Most of us know that spam is unwanted email. We also know that spam is a food product. Have you ever stopped to consider why the two are named alike?

SPAM, the lunch meat came first. Hormel introduced it in 1937, and it was an important part of Allied soldiers' meals. SPAM is precooked sliced pork; one can eat it straight from the can. SPAM stays fresh because of the canning process and because many preservatives and salts are added. Although Hormel says that SPAM – the proper spelling of the food is all capital letters - is not an acronym, people have suggested that someone may have intended to name it Shoulder of Pork And Ham at one time. Although not every soldier liked SPAM, many did, and when the troops settled back into family life, they insisted their grocery stores carry it. After World War II, SPAM became a part of many Americans' diets.

The personal computer became common in American homes in the 1990s, and shortly after that, unwanted bulk emails became known as spam. The concept of unwanted bulk electronic messages goes back way further than that; enterprising salespeople also used to send unwanted telegraph messages promoting products. The people before 1990 didn't call these unwanted bulk messages SPAM, so why did people in the 90s and after call it spam?

The British comedy troupe, Monty Python, can be thanked for that. In 1970, Monty Python performed a skit in which a woman in a restaurant attempted to order SPAM products. A group of Vikings in the restaurant heard her and began to sing, "SPAM, SPAM, SPAM." They sang so loud that the waiter could not hear the woman ordering. Because of that, loud, unwanted messages are known today as spam.

Hormel likely thought the fad would fade, but computer junk mail was still known as SPAM in the late 1990s. In 1998, Hormel took a public stand about unwanted bulk emails being referred to by its prize meat's name. Hormel stated that the company was fine with the public referring to the unwanted email as spam – all lowercase unless used as the first word of a sentence – as long as the general public always referred to their meat product with all capital letters . . . **SPAM.**

FUN FACTS

SPAM is often referred to as "mystery meat," but the ingredients in SPAM are much clearer than the ingredients in the typical hotdog.

George Hormel supposedly called it SPAM as slang for "spiced ham."

SPAM is very popular in the Pacific. Hawaii consumes more SPAM than any other state – it consumes over 7 million cans of SPAM per year, and, in the Philippines, there is a restaurant, SPAM Jam, that uses SPAM in all its dishes, including SPAM eggs and SPAM spaghetti.

CHAPTER 36

The Hoagie, the Grinder, and the Hero

Are you known by more than one name? Many people have a name people know them by, a full name, and a nickname. Consider Elizabeth Renee Cooper. Some people call her "Liz," some call her "Beth," and some say "Elizabeth". Others call her "Lizzie". When her dad is frustrated with her, he will say, "Elizabeth Renee." Some people know her as "Renee." Her peers call her "Coop," and her boyfriend calls her "Sweet Pea." On the first day of class, her teacher called her "Elizabeth Renee Cooper".

Some food items have the same issue. The same food is known by a lot of different names by a lot of different people, and yet it is the same food. For example, what do you call a sandwich made on a long cyclical roll instead of sliced bread or a rounded bun? Is it a "grinder," a "hoagie," an "Italian sandwich," a "po' boy," a "rocket," a "spukie," a "torpedo," a "Zephyr," a "Dagwood," or something else?

The different names reflect different traits of this sandwich. The first term in the above list refers to the people the sandwich was designed to feed. "Grinder" is slang for a dock worker who sands and repaints boat hulls. The sandwich was created for dockworkers in New England by Benedetto Capaldo, owner of the Sub Yard restaurant. The Sub Yard had a contract to provide 500 of the long sandwiches each day to the dock workers; the sandwich was praised by management for being simple to make and not messy to eat. People began to associate this sandwich with the grinder occupation.

The second name reflects who did the making and what the ingredients were; the third name references where it was made. The name "Italian sandwich" reflects that it was created by Italian immigrants for Italian immigrants around 1900; although it has spread worldwide, it is an American invention. The term "hoagie" reminds us that it was likely created on Hog Island, part of the Philadelphia Navy Yard; the sandwich was originally called a "hoggie," and that morphed into "hoagie."

Several names describe its appearance. The terms "rocket," "torpedo," and "Zephyr" all refer to its long oval shape, which looks like a rocket, torpedo, and blimp. The term "spukie" is Italian for a long, hard roll, which is what it was made from. Meanwhile, "Dagwood" reminds people that just about anything can be put on this long roll, which can be piled high, just as Dagwood Bumstead did in the comic strip Blondie. Similarly, the term "hero" reflects that this was a big sandwich and that only a man superior to most other men could eat it in one sitting.

Although this sandwich on a long cyclical roll began in the shipyards of New England, it rapidly moved elsewhere. Seafaring merchants who encountered the sandwich in New England went to other ports; people who enlisted in the Navy returned to their hometowns. The sandwich took root worldwide, but local cultures touched it uniquely. For instance, the sandwich found a home on the docks of the Gulf Coast of Louisiana, but instead of salami and similar meats, the dockworkers there insisted on seafood. When the Louisiana dock workers went on strike, the Louisiana version became known as the "po' boy" sandwich, supporting the financially strapped dock workers.

Grinders themselves didn't call the sandwich a "grinder"; they referred to them as "subs" because they came from the Sub Yard. Benedetto called both his restaurant and the sandwich after the boat whose shape the sandwich mimicked; he called the sandwich the **. . . submarine sandwich.**

FUN FACTS

The first commercial establishments to serve subs were Italian pizzerias.

Cornelius van Drebbel invented the first workable submarine in 1620; oars propelled it.

Submarines are more than military machines; they are used for scientific research, recreation, and search-and-rescue operations.

War itself may be terrible, but because so many soldiers passed through the naval bases serving submarine sandwiches, people around the nation learned about and loved the submarine sandwich when World War II ended.

CHAPTER 37

The Guest who Stole His Host's Recipes

    In 1709, Swedish King Charles XII had a problem. He had always thought of himself as a military genius. Having taken the throne at age 15, he had successfully subdued all his European enemies and begun the trek to Moscow, Russia. He had defeated the Russians in several battles, including one in which he was outnumbered three to one. However, on this day, Russia had regrouped and thrashed his army. He had been shot in the foot and could not lead the troops. To sum it up, the Swedes had been routed, and Russian troops blocked the road back to Sweden.

    Believing that the enemy of my enemy is my friend, Charles XII rushed to the border of the Ottoman Empire, a nation suspicious of the Russians. The Ottomans allowed Charles and his force of 1,000 to enter the country. Charles stayed in modern Turkey for almost five years, hoping to rebuild his troops and finish his goal of subduing Russia.

While in Turkey, Charles enjoyed Ottoman hospitality. Life moved at a slow, relaxed pace at the palace. When the palace staff wasn't spoiling him, he studied the Arab ships, leading him to create blueprints to advance Sweden's navy. Life was good. Charles would have stayed longer, but he received word that his homeland was attacked by an alliance of Russia, Hanover, Saxony, Great Britain, and Denmark. He hurried home and sought to restore order.

Charles was not known for being a foodie, but he and his men had been exposed to Turkish cooking. When they returned to Sweden, they still wanted to eat some of what they had eaten in Turkey. They craved coffee and cabbage rolls, two Turkish luxuries. They also craved meatballs; ground hamburger rolled into two-to-four-inch centimeter balls mixed with raw onions, beaten eggs, spices, and breadcrumbs soaked in milk. The Swedes had known of meatballs from the Italians. Still, these Turkish meatballs were smaller than Italian meatballs and had a very different taste sensation since they were soaked in brown gravy instead of tomato sauce.

The Swedish palace chefs could duplicate the Turkish recipe, and the king was very pleased. He was so pleased he showed off the dish at state dinners. The visiting statesmen generally knew nothing about Turkish cooking, so when they took the dish back to their own country, they called it . . . **Swedish meatballs.**

FUN FACTS

Turkish meatballs are usually made from lamb, but Swedish meatballs are made from beef or pork.

Swedish meatballs are usually served with boiled or mashed potatoes, gravy, and lingonberry jam.

In Turkey, there are a variety of meatballs, each named for the city that supposedly created it.

CHAPTER 38
The Food Named After Gunpowder

Have you ever noticed how different people eat different foods in different regions of the country? For instance, if you want biscuits and gravy, fried okra, and sweet tea in the United States, you must go down South. Each state may be considered part of the United States, but its citizens eat very differently.

Likewise, Mexican culture varies from one region to another. By 1492, Mexican regional cultures had shared the technology to ground wheat and corn to make tortilla shells. However, what the cooks put in those shells varied significantly from region to region. Some regional cultures had vegetables, some had meat, and some had a little of both; none had warm ground hamburgers covered by cool lettuce, cheese, tomatoes, and sour cream, all served in a warm shell.

When the Spanish sailed to Mexico and subdued it, they found the various yummies wrapped in the round shell; they noticed the wrapped pack looked like a Spanish tarte, so they called the unleavened flatbread a "tortilla," the Spanish word for "tarte."

As the United States expanded Westward, many Mexicans migrated from their rural farms to the United States, working at ranches, building railroads, and settling into the inner cities as street vendors. The Mexican immigrants brought the tarte and other food with them; Americans liked the Mexican foods, but they adjusted the spiciness to suit themselves.

Before the 1960s, Mexican food in the United States was generally made to order. The street vendor or Mexican restaurant would provide a soft tortilla shell, and the patron would specify which ingredients and how much of each ingredient to put in. In the 1960s, though, people wanted faster service, which meant having items premade for consumers. Mexican food started to join hamburgers as fast food when Taco Bell developed a recipe for a hard, precooked shell. The precooked shell solved the problem of tartes getting mushy, allowing Taco Bell to make up the orders beforehand. Taco Bell set a standard design for the tartes - warm grounded hamburger covered by cool lettuce, cheese, tomatoes, and sour cream, all served in a warm shell; the United States accepted this, and Taco Bell and its competitors have sold the Mexican dish this Americanized way ever since.

What is this delicacy with over 4000 years of history in Central and South America and over 100 years in the United States? Believe it or not, the Spanish named this dish after gunpowder. The Spanish were using small round packages of gunpowder to mine silver to take back to Spain; because the food in the tortilla was also small, round, and packed a punch – thanks to the peppers, the Spanish called the Mexican food the same thing they called the gunpowder packets . . . **tacos.** (Believe it or not, although the Mexicans use many terms for their tortilla dishes, "taco" is not one of them. However, they use the word "taco" to describe the American dish.)

FUN FACTS

The restaurant that would become Taco Bell in 1962 was started in 1950 as Bell's Hamburgers and Shakes by Glen W. Bell in San Bernardino, California.

In the United States, October 4 is National Taco Day: National Taco Day is celebrated in Mexico every March 31.

Two women in New York operated the first taco food truck in 1966.

PART FOUR:
DESSERTS AND CANDIES

CHAPTER 39

Johnny Appleseed was Johnny Come Lately

All hail the crab apple tree! Even though its fruit is generally too bitter to be eaten raw, let us honor it now. Let us hail it because the North American continent would not have had any apple trees without it until European migration began in the late 1600s.

The Europeans who settled in the United States have been stereotyped as religious zealots or greedy land grabbers. Still, some were scientists interested in exploring the New World's soil. These scientists/settlers at Jamestown, the first permanent colonial settlement in what would become the United States, brought their own apple trees to plant. Although it would take years for them to produce fruit, the scientists hoped to feed future generations of settlers. To their satisfaction, the apple trees flourished in the new land.

A little over 100 years later, America had become an independent nation and had begun to move Westward. Young Johnny Chapman may not have had a botany degree, but he also realized that if someone would go ahead of the pioneers and plant apple trees, "no one would ever go hungry." Not seeing anyone racing for the job, he decided to go himself, establishing nurseries and exchanging saplings for supplies from Pennsylvania through Ohio.

Johnny was a pleasurable, memorable fellow. He dressed simply, wearing a tin pot as a hat and a burlap sack belted around him. He was a Christian environmentalist and would tell anyone who would listen about both if anyone had an interest in listening; he believed that everyone should be a good steward of planet Earth. He traveled light, relying on the generosity of others for food and lodging. However, he had a giving spirit, and if settlers couldn't afford to buy apple seeds or an apple tree sapling from him, he would give them a sapling.

By 1822, people were fondly calling him "Johnny Appleseed." Today, many of the apple trees in the United States can trace their roots back to a tree that Johnny planted.

If you grew up in the United States, you likely heard this story in elementary school. There are three important details, though, that teachers usually do not share with young ears. You're older now, so I will share them with you. Fact One, many of the apples from the tree were used for hard apple cider; many American frontiersmen had a drinking problem, and the Prohibition Movement would wrestle with this social issue in upcoming years. Fact Two, Johnny may have dressed in burlap and relied on the generosity of others, but he made a fortune by establishing nurseries, leaving them with someone to tend, and then coming back to collect his share of the profits. Fact Three, it was the British, long before the colonies even thought about becoming a nation, that came up with one of the best recipes for apples . . . **the apple pie.**

FUN FACTS

Crab apple trees make great firewood.

Crab apple trees work as pollinizers for other apple trees, and many apple orchards will have every sixth or seventh row dedicated to crab apple trees because of this.

Today the United States is one of the world's largest producers of apples.

The American Pie Council has determined that apple pie is the favorite pie of the United States.

CHAPTER 40

The Food, the Flavor, the Memory

Before reading this article, I want you to take a sheet of paper and make a paper cylinder. Now, look at that cylinder closely. What would it have to do if something wanted to get into the cylinder on the side? That's right; it would have to enter at the seam.

That cylinder is how primitive people like the Druids, the original residents of much of Western Europe, understood the world. They believed that as one year joined up with another year, beings from the other side could get into the world through the seam. One of the reasons we dress up on Halloween is to blend in with any ghosts visiting from the other side, for their old year ended October 31, and the new began on November 1.

Not only did the earth complete a cycle each year, but so did a person. They carefully marked the day each person was born, fearing that evil spirits from the other side could enter that person's world on their birthday. To keep the evil spirits away, people would gather around the birthday person and make a lot of noise. These sessions eventually evolved into parties with organized songs, games, and noisemakers. Although the birthday party was to honor the person, more importantly, it was to keep them safe.

The concept of having a cake to honor somebody comes from an ancient Greek ritual to the moon goddess. People would honor her with a cake with candles, which represented stars. People began honoring other people with cake too. Birthdays were an occasion to honor someone with a cake, and typically one candle was placed on the cake for each year the person was, plus an extra one to grow on.

Any cake was considered a birthday cake until 1989. Chocolate, angel food, red velvet, carrot – you name it; if it was a cake, it was acceptable as a birthday cake. In 1989, though, things began to change. That year Pillsbury introduced Funfetti, artificial sugar sprinkles that were designed to be put on cakes. Pillsbury showed Funfetti being applied to a white vanilla cake with buttercream icing. Parents and kids alike embraced the idea of that – and only that - being a birthday cake.

Now that the definition of birthday cake had been limited to one type of cake, manufacturers started to make flavored treats such as doughnuts and ice cream, lip gloss, and even candles with the vanilla-like scent associated with the cake. Most people readily recognized the scent and found it comforting, a friend from the past. You probably won't be surprised to learn that they called this unique smell **. . . birthday cake.**

FUN FACTS

Funfetti are flavorless; they are purely decoration.

Before 1989, there was no such word as "Funfetti". "Funfetti" is a word that Pillsbury invented by blending the words "fun" and "confetti".

The first box cake mix was created in 1930 by John D. Duff; it was a gingerbread cake.

Although no one is certain, the Egyptians were likely the first to bake cakes; they made honey-sweet dessert breads.

For its 100th anniversary, Oreo cookies decorated their centers with Funfetti, which was birthday cake flavored.

CHAPTER 41

Food Designed to Teach

Have you ever witnessed a children's Christmas program at a church? In many of these programs, the children will sit together in the choir loft or a pew. When it is time, they will sing carols and act out the story of the birth of Christ. After the play, the minister will address the congregation, either giving a benediction or launching into a full sermon.

Kids have a hard time sitting through a sermon. The choirmaster at Cologne Cathedral in Germany knew this. He had dealt with rowdy kids the past few Christmas seasons, and many of those same children were in his choir again this year, 1620. Parents would scowl when he couldn't control their kids, and the preacher would glare at him as the kids talked and smacked each other.

This year, though, the choirmaster was ready. He had brought some peppermint sticks with him. He believed that the desire to have a peppermint would inspire the children to behave and that once they had the candy in their mouths, they would not talk. Although his reasons for bringing the peppermints were pragmatic, he knew that the pastor would not want the boys to be eating candy in church.

Therefore, he also used the peppermint stick as a teaching tool. He asked the local candy maker to make the peppermint stick with a 180-degree curve at the end; this bend made it appear as a miniature shepherd staff, a reminder that shepherds went to the manager to see The Lamb of God. The candy was a white stick; the white was to remind the boys that Jesus had never sinned and that he was pure. In years ahead, other people carried on this tradition, turning the product upside down and declaring that the resulting "J" was for Jesus. They added three red stripes, the three representing the Trinity – Father, Son, and Holy Spirit - and the red representing the saving blood of Jesus. They also pointed out that the candy was hard, for Christ was the rock upon which they should build their lives.

The boys behaved very well that day in church, and the passing out of the candy shepherd's crooks became a Christmas tradition picked up by Christian congregations worldwide. Although they may have looked like shepherd's crooks, people called them "bent candy sticks" until 1866 because almost all candy sticks were long since bending them was tedious. This changed in 1866 when a machine was invented that could bend them. Although the bent shape still reminded people of a shepherd's crook, it looked even more like a cane, so people began to call the treat . . . **the candy cane.**

FUN FACTS

Candy canes came in one color for over 200 years – white.

In the 1950s, Gregory Keller, a seminary student who worked summers at his brother-in-law's candy shop in Atlanta, Georgia, invented a machine that allowed candy canes to be produced quickly; Bob McCormack – you may have heard of Bob's Candies – took his brother-in-law's invention and commercialized the candy cane.

Although the traditional candy cane is white with red stripes and tastes of peppermint, today, candy canes are available in various colors and tastes.

Candy canes are not just for eating. They can be hung to decorate Christmas trees or taped to packages as decorations.

Although peppermint sticks and candy canes are available year-round, they are in high demand at Christmas.

CHAPTER 42
A Good Cook Had an Off Day – and It Changed Her Life

Good cooks can make everything but one thing – a mistake. Good cooks do not make mistakes!

Ruth Graves Wakefield was a good cook; no, she was an excellent cook. People came for miles to dine at her Toll House Inn in Whitman, Massachusetts. She and her husband had run the inn for several years; he did the upkeep, and she oversaw the cooking. The Toll House Inn was known for the home-cooked meals it served in the restaurant and the food it served its guests.

One of the things Ruth did was fix a late-night dessert for her guests. One of her favorite desserts was ice cream with homemade Butter Drop Do cookies, thin butterscotch nut cookies. Ruth was usually organized, but she was short of baker's chocolate that evening. In a tizzy, she took a chocolate candy bar, cut it into small chunks, and scattered the chunks into the cookie dough. She then baked the cookies as usual, expecting the chocolate to melt into the dough. (A good cook would know this would not work, and Ruth was a good cook, so she never confessed that she had gotten into a tizzy.)

Imagine her shock when she pulled the cookies out of the oven and discovered the chocolate shavings hadn't melted. The small chocolate shavings had gotten warm and gooey but didn't melt. Ruth didn't have time to cook anything else, so she put the cookies on a plate and took them to her guests. She thought fast and said, "I made some Toll House Chocolate Crunch Cookies. I hope you like them."

The guests didn't like them – they loved them! Ruth realized she had stumbled onto something wonderful. Since it was a Nestle candy bar that she had chopped up, she excitedly called the Nestle company to see if they would be interested in purchasing the recipe. They were. They agreed to give her a lifetime supply of chocolate for the rights to the recipe and the Toll House name.

Ruth took them up on the offer. Ruth's fame and that of the cookie spread rapidly. She published the recipe in her cookbook *Toll House Tried and True Recipes* in 1938. The recipe was also featured on the Betty Crocker Cooking School radio show. In 1939, Nestle began making "chocolate morsels," candy bar pieces already cut up and ready for putting into cookies. Nestle then started to print the recipe on the back of its chocolate chip packages, which is still published today.

FUN FACTS

The chocolate chip cookie is the state cookie of Massachusetts, where it was invented.

Many hotels, such as Double Tree Inns, serve chocolate chip cookies to their guests. Not only are these a welcome treat to the guests, but they also keep the hotel smelling terrific.

Betty Crocker was a marketing character; there was no real Betty Crocker. The person who played Betty Crocker on the radio, Marjorie Child Husted, was the inventor of the character.

The Wakefields ran the Toll House Inn until they sold it in 1966. The Toll House Inn burned to the ground in 1984; today, an ice cream restaurant stands where it did, and a plaque marks the historical site.

CHAPTER 43

A Failed Industrial Invention Became a Hit Dessert with Flavoring and Marketing

Do you remember learning about Peter Cooper in grade school? Peter Cooper invented the Tom Thumb, the first railroad steam engine in the United States. Cooper's invention was a major step in the evolution of the steam engine used for rail transportation and the steam engine used in the Industrial Revolution; his steam engine changed history.

Like many other inventors, Peter Cooper didn't invent just one thing in his lifetime; he invented many things. One of his most overlooked inventions was powdered gelatin. Peter's powdered gelatin was made of animal byproducts – beef hooves, bones, and fat. It was tasteless and odorless, but it was a great gelling agent. Peter patented gelatin in 1845, but unlike some of his inventions, this one did not catch on with the public – at that time.

People like Pearle Wait, a cough-syrup manufacturer, experimented with the gelatin. He found that by adding sugar and cherry flavoring to it, he had a tasty dessert. He and his wife soon had orange, lemon, strawberry, and raspberry flavors. Pearle, though, didn't have the money to promote the tasty dessert, so he sold his recipe to Frank Woodward, the owner of Genesee Food Company, the company which became General Foods in 1900.

By 1902, Frank was ready to mass produce the product. He tried promoting the dessert in the *Ladies Home Journal*, a women's magazine, claiming it was "America's Most Famous Dessert." (The adage "Fake it until you make it" certainly applies here because it was neither famous nor the favorite.) Women, though, were not overly inspired to try it.

Frank didn't give up on the product. He chose six flavors to sell - cherry, grape, lemon-lime, orange, raspberry, and strawberry, and then set about to market his product in a way that had never been done; he had his marketing team assemble a cookbook with numerous recipes using the flavored gelatin and then proceeded to give away thousands of copies of the book throughout the nation. The recipe book was quality with Norman Rockwell's art, so people welcomed it and its recipes into their homes. The recipes showed how the product could be used to create salads and combined with celery, green peppers, and pasta; the food looked good, and people tried them.

Today, the flavored powdered gelatin is still used to make salads and desserts and to add flavoring to other foods. It also has other uses, such as hair dye and finger paint. Not only are there original powdered gelatin cartons, but General Foods also manufactures pudding and frozen desserts in the gelatin flavors.

Frank kept the product's name exactly as Pearle had sold it to him, and Pearle kept it with the name his wife, May, had come up with. When her husband showed her his experiments, she marveled at how Peter's invention gelled – "gell, oooh", so she named it . . . **Jell-o.**

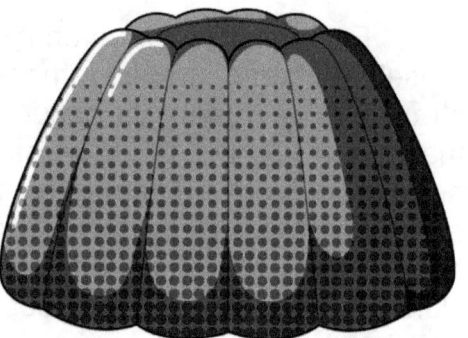

FUN FACTS

Jell-o is often given to children who have upset stomachs.

The top-selling flavor of Jell-o is strawberry.

Jell-o is almost 90% sugar.

Although known for its fruit flavors, Jell-o has tried – and discontinued – vegetable flavors such as celery.

CHAPTER 44

Which Came First – Lemon Pie or Lime Pie?

Which came first, the lemon pie or the lime pie?

Most people would say you are correct if you said the lemon pie. In 1931, the Borden Milk Company in New York shared the recipe with the public. This sharing wasn't necessarily because Borden loved pie and couldn't keep the creation of lemon pie to itself – although that may be true; it was because a major ingredient in the lemon pie is sweetened condensed milk, a product that Borden produced.

Borden shared the recipe with the national press, and people around the nation began to enjoy lemon pie. The recipe made it to Florida, where an enterprising cook substituted limes, a traditional Florida fruit, for the lemons. According to these scholars, the lemon pie came first.

But did it? Although the pro-lemon people showed that the recipe appeared in New York before recipes for lime pie appeared in Florida, there may be more to the story. Remember I told you that Borden released the recipe? Let me ask you, where did it get the recipe? The pro-lemon faction will say that a Borden employee wrote it. The pro-lime faction has a different story.

The pro-lime faction claims that Borden obtained the recipe by sponsoring a recipe contest. People from around the nation sent in recipes. They contend that a Floridian sent in a recipe for lime pie, and Borden substituted lemons for limes.

Lime pie was created by a lady now known as Aunt Sally; she was the cook for William Curry's family. William was a ship salvager who had become a millionaire and possibly learned the recipe from a sponge fisherman from the Florida Keys. Aunt Sally supposedly made the first lime pie in 1880. She didn't bother to write down the recipe, but the pie became a family favorite. One of her guests was so impressed that the guest sent the recipe to Borden, who changed limes for lemons and then found its way back to Florida, where the lemons were changed back to limes.

Regardless of where the recipe came from, there is no doubt that the lemon pie originated in New York and the lime pie in Florida. The people who named the lime pie paid tribute to Aunt Sally and the Curry mansion, naming the pie . . . **Key Lime Pie.**

FUN FACTS

Mexican limes, also known as West Indian limes, were transplanted into Key West Florida, resulting in Key limes. The words "Key lime" pay tribute to the birthplace and the type of lime used.

Key lime pie is made from the fruit of the lime tree; the leaves can be used to make stews and curries.

In 2006, Key lime pie was named the official pie of Florida.

CHAPTER 45
A Chocolate Maker's Alternative to Messy Chocolate

Have you ever stared up at the clouds and shared what you saw? A cloud may have reminded you of a dragon, a car, or a horse. Like a psychologist's ink-spot test in which the shapes can be anything, most of us often clearly recognize specific forms when none was intended.

Clarence Crane was the son of a wealthy maple sugar farmer. He worked for his dad, learned about the business, and started his own maple syrup company in 1903. It, too, proved very successful; in 1909, he sold it but kept working for it. In 1911, he found his true passion, making chocolate.

Clarence invested his savings in his latest idea. He opened the Queen Victoria Chocolate Company in 1911. By 1912, he was a well-respected, established chocolate manufacturer in Cleveland, Ohio. The summer of 1912, though, was an extremely hot one in Cleveland, and Clarence was concerned because sales were down since the summer heat melted the chocolate so quickly. He wanted to give his patrons a candy treat they could enjoy on hot days, so he created a round peppermint mint with a hole in the middle. However, not having the time or the space to mass produce his creation, Clarence turned to a local pill manufacturer to produce the treat.

His patrons loved the Pep-o-Mint. One of his customers was Edward Noble, the creator of the ABC radio network. Edward believed the Pep-o-Mint would be appreciated outside of Cleveland; he even believed it could become an international treat. Edward ran by many ideas for new flavors and marketing this round mint with a hole in it, but Clarence was happy with life as it was. Nobel saw the potential, so he kept making suggestions; finally, Clarence sold him the rights to make and sell the Pep-o-Mint.

Noble carried through with his ideas. He retained the peppermint flavor but added new ones like wintergreen and chocolate. One of his biggest hits occurred in 1925 when he introduced cherry-flavored mints and other "fruit drops with a hole" in their center. By 1935, he also had orange, pineapple, lime, and lemon flavors and even packaged the five together and separately.

The candy was a very unusual shape for its time. In the early 1900s, the European mints imported into the United States were pillow-shaped; Clarence settled on the round shape to distinguish his candy mint as American. He further distinguished it by putting a hole in the center to complement the "O" in the name – Pep-o-Mint. (Urban myth would later say that Clarence placed the hole in the mint because his son had choked to death on a mint, but Clarence's only son, Hart, was alive and well.) When Clarence looked at his creation, he saw a lifebuoy, and so he named his candy . . . **the Life Saver.**

CHAPTER 46
Chocolate that Melts in Your Mouth – Not Your Hand

One of the problems with chocolate is that it melts at a low temperature. In the days before refrigeration and air conditioning, this was a big concern, and even today, chocolate that melts in one's hand is not very pleasurable. Chocolate makers were very aware of this problem, and while some tried to find other treats for their clients during the hot summer months, others tried to find a way to sell chocolates year-round.

Forrest E. Mars, Sr., the son of the legendary candy manufacturer Frank C. Mars who had founded the Mars candy company, was in this latter group. By 29, Forrest had already invented the Snickers and Three Musketeers bars. Forrest discovered the hard way that owning a candy company was more than just about inventing new products; he and his father had a major disagreement about marketing strategy, and Forrest, who wanted to do international marketing, found himself on his own. Forrest accepted a buyout from his father and then moved to England, where he started his own company. There, he introduced the Mars bar and Maltesers.

An American at heart, Forrest still cared about his new countrymen. Although England was officially neutral in the Spanish Civil War, many people from England voluntarily participated in it. Forrest wanted to check on these soldiers and see what he, a sweets purveyor, could do to make their time in the service more enjoyable. While mingling with the troops, he came across a candy from a rival company, Rowntree of York, a Smartie. Invented in 1937, the Smartie had a tough, colored shell with chocolate inside. Forrest studied how the shell had been formed, then moved back to the United States, taking the idea with him.

He noticed that hardened sugar syrup on the outside could protect the chocolate inside so that the candy would not melt upon contact with one's hand. Frank improved on the process and secured a U.S. patent in March 1941. Forrest approached Bruce Murrie, the son of the president of Hershey's chocolate, William F.R. Murrie, about being his partner; this partnership ensured that Forrest would have a steady supply of chocolate to make his latest design, a candy with a hard shell and a chocolate center, even with chocolate being rationed. They sold a lot of candy those first four years – but it was all to the military; just as the British had learned in the Spanish Civil War, the chocolate with a special shell could survive being in the warm outdoors or in being carried in pockets, so it was the ideal chocolate for soldiers. After the war ended, Forrest and William were allowed to sell the candy to the general public. With the war over and chocolate readily available, Forrest bought out William's share and became the sole owner of the candy.

Forrest continued to tinker with the product's image. In 1948, he began to sell the candy in easily recognizable brown bags. Facing competition from generic companies, in 1950, Forrest began to put a black "M" on each piece of candy to reassure the public it was the real thing. In 1954, the "M" became white. If you are wondering why the letter "M" and not something else, it is because Forrest was using the initial of his last name, "Mars." He had named the product after himself and Murrie, calling it the . . . **M & M.**

FUN FACTS

Peanut M&Ms were introduced in 1954, a peanut covered with chocolate and a special syrup coating. They appeared only in tan for the first six years, and then green, red, and yellow colors were added.

The original M&M became known as the plain M&M because new flavors were tried. Mint, almond, hazelnut, coffee toffee, peanut butter, and pretzel are just six of the many flavors M&Ms have been available in, but nothing has ever surpassed the sales of the plain and peanut flavors.

The anthropomorphic peanut M&M and the plain anthropomorphic M&M both came into existence in 1950; they could be seen diving into a pool of chocolate.

Upon his dad's death, Forrest merged his M&M company with the Mars Company he had run in his twenties.

In 1981, M&Ms became the first candy in outer space, part of the meal served to the Columbia space crew.

M&Ms originally came in five colors – brown, green, purple, red, and yellow.

CHAPTER 47

"A Snack as Big as the Moon"

What do you think of when you think of a coal mine? If you're like me, you think of coal. You also think of a dark, damp, dank place. For most people, it's not the place to get ideas for new food items.

Earl Mitchell, a traveling salesman for the Chattanooga Bakery in Chattanooga, Tennessee, in 1912, would disagree. Earl wanted to make sales, and one of the best ways to make sales is to find out what potential customers want and then give it to them. When he looked at the coal miners, he didn't see filth-covered men; he saw people who needed to eat – and he wanted to be the one to provide them their food.

Therefore, Earl went to the coal miners and bluntly asked the miners what they wanted. They gave him strange ideas, such as "a snack as big as the moon." Earl knew he couldn't make one literally the size of the moon, but he understood the man to mean that he wanted a really, really big snack. Earl could do that.

Earl returned to the bakery with his idea for "a snack as big as the moon." The bakery sold over 100 items, but none fit that description. The Chattanooga Bakery created a large, filling snack using graham crackers, chocolate, and marshmallows. It may not have been literally as big as the moon, but it filled the full length of a large lunch pail, and, at a mere nickel, it was not only big and filling but also affordable.

Today the treat comes in a standard 4" size. Chocolate remains a favorite, although vanilla, strawberry, banana, and other flavors are available. Miniature versions are available, and so are double – even triple-deckers. The food is found worldwide but sells best in the South. Whereas New York has a ball fall every New Year's Eve at the stroke of midnight, in Mobile, Alabama, a lighted mechanical version of this treat is dropped 34 stories to bring in the New Year. Southerners love this out-of-the-world treat and honor its big-as-the-moon heritage, calling it . . . **the MoonPie.**

FUN FACTS

The original MoonPie was too light to sell in a vending machine, so a second layer was added.

The MoonPie has the same ingredients as a s'more – chocolate, graham crackers, and marshmallows, just in different proportions.

The MoonPie has often been paired with an RC Cola; during the Great Depression, each was five cents and made for a great meal on the go.

CHAPTER 48
The Edible Flag

When I go out of town for an extended period, I like to take something that reminds me of home. It might be a keepsake; it might be a picture. Seeing a memento of home helps me to relax.

The Italian immigrants coming to the United States in the 1870s felt the same. They were proud Americans, but they still took comfort in seeing reminders of their native land. Many Italians came from Naples, a center for frozen desserts. When they came to the United States, ice cream stands and frozen desserts in confectionary stores were rare, and many Italians filled this void by opening an ice cream shop.

Italians welcomed the red, white, and blue of the United States and gladly accepted the stars and stripes as their own. However, they still had a fondness for the red, white, and green stripes of their native country. If you have ever seen the Italian flag, then you know that one-third of the Italian flag is red, one-third is white, and one-third is green.

The Italians combined the love of their flag with their love of ice cream, creating an ice cream treat in which one-third was green ice cream, one-third was white, and one-third was red. When the carton was opened, their native flag was staring at them.

Three flavors parallel to each other in one carton was not a new sight to the Italians; the recipe had been written in 1839, but it was around long before that. Although Americans credited the Italians with inventing the concept of putting three flavors in one container, the person who shared the recipe in 1839 was the head chef of Louis Ferdinand Jungius, Prussian royalty.

The three flavors in one container had many advantages. The ice cream container was practical for feeding family members with varying tastes; a household just needed one carton instead of three. Also, it gave people a choice; people could have one of the three flavors exclusively or have some of each.

The three flavors the Italians chose to put into the one carton - pistachio (green), vanilla (white), and cherry (red) - were not a hit with Americans. Sales were modest at best. Americans liked chocolate, vanilla, and strawberry. In the 1860s, an enterprising Italian American decided to substitute chocolate for pistachio, keep vanilla for the white, and use strawberry for the red. The concept of chocolate, vanilla, and strawberry together in one carton was an American innovation. Although the Italians called the three flavors parallel to each other "spumoni," Americans who ate the chocolate/vanilla/strawberry combination named it after the immigrants from Naples, Italy, whom they called Neapolitans, calling it . . . **Neapolitan ice cream.**

Although Neapolitan refers to a chocolate/vanilla/strawberry combination of ice cream, it can also be applied to any three-layer dessert.

In Italy, spumoni often has a layer of fruits and nuts between each layer of ice cream.

The Italian flag, affectionately nicknamed the "tricolor," must be flown with the green vertical stripe closest to the hoist and the red vertical stripe farthest from it.

CHAPTER 49
Perfection Every Time

In the 1890s, Charles Cretors was the proud owner of a confectionary shop in Decatur, Illinois. Charles would have been insulted if you called his store a mere candy store, for he sold all kinds of tempting sweets in addition to candy. In fact, over the years, his store had evolved from being a bakery to being about sweets in general.

Charles was open to new products. In the early 1890s, he added roasted nuts that he personally roasted. He had purchased a steam-powered machine that would perfectly cook the nuts. At least, it was supposed to do that. Charles was unhappy with the product, so he started to tinker with it. Before long, he had built his own nut-roasting machine.

Charles continued to tinker with the steam engine, finding ways to roast other products. One day in 1885, he successfully roasted corn kernels that would expand and puff when heated in oil. This may not sound like much initially, but this was big news!

What Charles observed that day in 1885 was not a scientific breakthrough. The concept of heating corn in oil until it popped had been discovered by people in Peru over 4,400 years before. Many people in Charles' town heated corn over the fire until its kernel expanded to 20-50 times its original size. Families enjoyed both making and eating the corn.

What Charles had created with his steam engine was a way to get the popped corn to taste the same way batch after batch. When people tried to make their own, they were just as likely to get it too dark or uncooked as they were to get it just right. If a batch cooked too slowly, the water in the kernel would seep out, and the kernel would never pop; if the water heated too quickly, the kernel would explode but be hard and chewy.

Charles knew he had a winner on his hands, both food-wise and invention-wise. He quickly patented his steam engine. Before long, street carts could be found in most American communities cooking popped corn. By 1900, he was manufacturing horse-drawn carts as well. When electricity became available, Charles began to use electric motors.

Although Charles was not the person to discover the tasty treat, Charles was the one who figured out how to cook it consistently so that each batch was just as good as the previous batch. The smell of the popped corn or the roasted peanuts was all the advertising the product needed.

It might surprise you to know that not everyone liked Charles' food. Snobbish theater owners in the 1920s, in particular, found that when they served it at their concession stands that it distracted people from the movie. The theater owners were marketing movies to high-brow people - one had to read the captions to enjoy silent films – and popped corn was looked upon as a snack of the lower class. However, they lost their refined taste when they realized that sales of popped corn were higher than ticket sales, and movies and popped corn have been associated ever since.

If you had gone to Charles' store in 1885, you could have asked for "popped corns," "popcorns," or pop-corn, and he probably would have figured out that you wanted what he called . . . **popcorn.**

FUN FACTS

Popcorn isn't just to eat. You can string it and wrap it around a Christmas tree. Strings like beads can also be hung vertically in doorway entrances to create walls.

A single popped kernel of corn is a "flake."

In 1981, General Mills introduced microwave popcorn.

Although the Native Americans were the guest of the pilgrims on the first Thanksgiving, they brought food to share; one of the dishes they brought was popcorn.

CHAPTER 50
A Soldier's Best Friend

Picture the coldest day that you have ever seen; a day that is so cold that even the engines of Jeeps crack; picture it being literally 30 to 40 degrees below zero Fahrenheit (negative 34.4 to 40 Celsius); picture it being so cold that you can't get your food container opened because the lid is frozen shut. Because of the weather, supplies cannot be brought in by land. However, enemy soldiers prepared for this terrain are approaching and threatening to encircle you, cutting you off from any reinforcements or supplies; the enemy soldiers outnumber you and your friends ten to one. Suddenly, unannounced, a friendly plane appears overhead through the cold and gloom and begins to drop pallets full of wooden cases. As these crates parachute to the ground safely, how would you feel?

This happened to American soldiers during the Korean War. On one of the coldest days of the year, they found themselves in dire straits, with the Chinese and Korean forces surrounding them in rural winter terrain. When the plane dropped the pallets, though, the soldiers' moods became optimistic, none more so than the mood of the commanding officer. The commander believed those crates contained the mortar shells he had radioed for, and his soldiers would have the ammunition they needed to keep the enemy a safe distance away. The commander's mood went from hope to shock to despair in a matter of moments, though, for when the pallets were opened, it was discovered that they did not contain ammunition; the crates were full of one-inch pellets of chocolate taffy candy, tiny little Tootsie Rolls.

The supply sergeant shook his head in disbelief, mumbling, "Tootsie Rolls." He immediately realized what had happened: "Tootsie Rolls" was the code name for 60 mm mortar shells, but somebody back at the American headquarters had thought he had ordered crates of literal Tootsie Rolls. He was racking his brain to determine what to say in response to this error when he noticed that the soldiers were joyfully snacking on the Tootsie Rolls; they hadn't been able to eat all day, and this childhood treat provided an excellent source of calories.

He couldn't help but notice, too, that a couple of the fast-thinking, creative soldiers in the unit had begun to experiment with the candy. They verified that the candy could be heated quickly and reformed into a different shape; they further observed that in the 40-below weather, the candy froze again quickly, retaining that shape. The soldiers melted the Tootsie rolls and used them as putty to patch bullet holes in barrels and mechanical parts in their Jeeps. With the soldiers rejuvenated and their vehicles working again, the commander led the men in an organized retreat to safety and to a time of regrouping.

When Leo Hirschfield invented the Tootsie Roll in 1907, he never dreamed that his candy would be what kept those U.S. Marines alive that day in Chosen Reservoir in North Korea almost fifty years later. He was an Austrian Jewish immigrant just trying to make candy for young and old people to enjoy.

He succeeded. The candy was an instant hit with both parents and children. Not only did parents like the taste, but they also loved the no-mess of the Tootsie Roll; meanwhile, kids loved the price of a mere penny - and both loved the taste of his chocolate taffy. To further establish a family-friendly aura around his chocolate taffy, Leo chose a name for his product that made people think of his own family; he named the candy after his daughter, Clara, the one he called **. . . Tootsie.**

FUN FACTS

Tootsie Rolls have been certified as kosher by the Orthodox Union.

Tootsie Rolls were the first individually-wrapped penny candy in the United States.

Approximately 64 million Tootsie Rolls are produced each day.

The Korean War was not the only war in which the U.S. government provided Tootsie Rolls as rations for its soldiers; it also provided them in both World War I and World War II.

Did you enjoy the book?

If you did, we are ecstatic. If not, please write your complaint to us and we will ensure we fix it.

If you're feeling generous, there is something important that you can help me with – tell other people that you enjoyed the book.

Ask a grown-up to write about it on Amazon. When they do, more people will find out about the book. It also lets Amazon know that we are making kids around the world laugh. Even a few words and ratings would go a long way.

If you have any ideas or jokes that you think are super funny, please let us know. We would love to hear from you. Our email address is -

riddleland@riddlelandforkids.com

Other Fun Books By Riddleland
Riddles Series

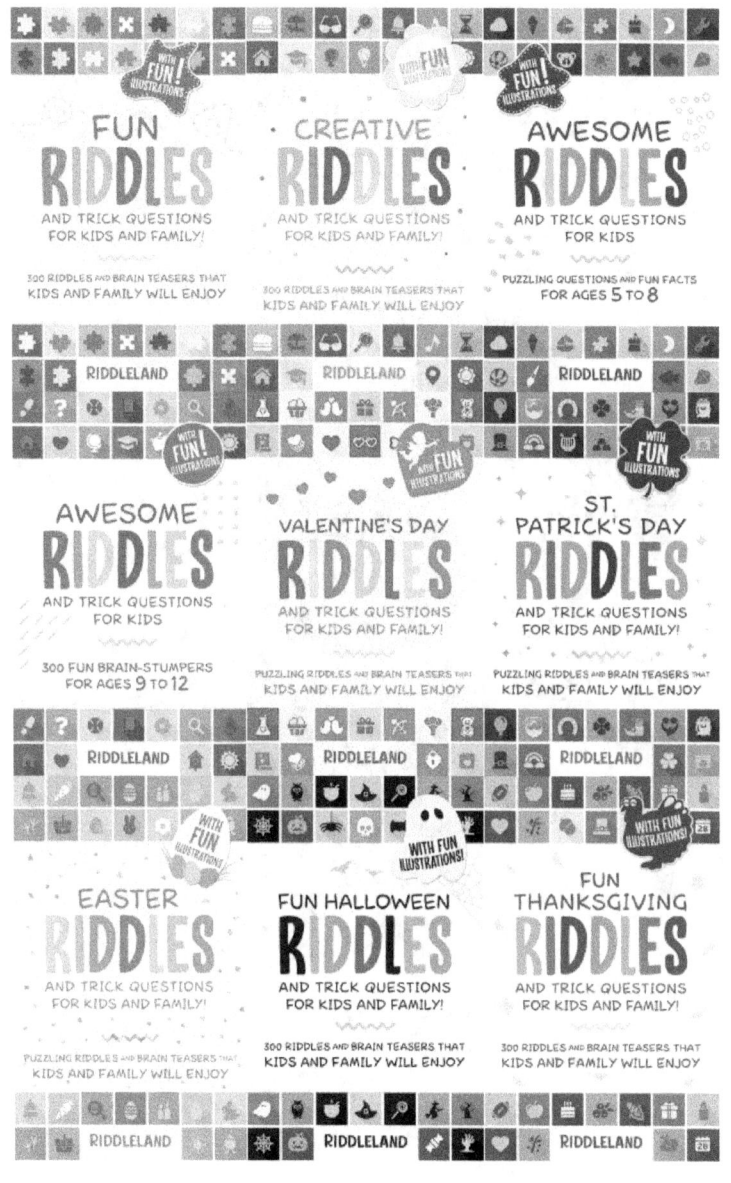

Its Laugh O'Clock Joke Books

It's Laugh O'Clock Would You Rather Books

**Get them on Amazon
or our website at www.riddlelandforkids.com**

About Riddleland

Riddleland is a mum + dad run publishing company. We are passionate about creating fun and innovative books to help children develop their reading skills and fall in love with reading. If you have suggestions for us or want to work with us, shoot us an email at

riddleland@riddlelandforkids.com

Our family's favorite quote:

"Creativity is an area in which younger people
have a tremendous advantage since
they have an endearing habit of always
questioning past wisdom and authority."
~ Bill Hewlett

Riddleland Bonus

Join our Facebook Group at Riddleland
For Kids to get daily jokes and riddles.

Bonus Book

https://pixelfy.me/riddlelandbonus

Thank you for buying this book. As a token of our appreciation, we would like to offer a special bonus a- collection of 50 original jokes, riddles, and funny stories.